SIMON EVANS
his life and later work

by

Mark Baldwin

B

M & M Baldwin
Cleobury Mortimer, Shropshire
1992

ISBN 0 947712 17 8

Published by M & M Baldwin
24 High Street, Cleobury Mortimer, Kidderminster DY14 8BY

Keyboarded by Electronic Office
4 Talbot Square, Cleobury Mortimer, Kidderminster DY14 8BQ

Printed by Severnside Printers Ltd., Upton-on-Severn, Worcestershire

CONTENTS

INTRODUCTION

Simon Evans, one of Shropshire's best-known literary figures, left little material for a biography amongst his published work. Although most of his writing stems directly from his own experience, and provides occasional personal insights, it is not genuinely autobiographical. It must be borne in mind that when authors appear to be writing about themselves, they do not always provide the unadorned and complete truth. I have therefore gleaned from Evans' books and articles such personal details as these appear to offer, but have supplemented and corroborated these details from other sources wherever possible.* Nevertheless, some of my conclusions must remain open to debate.

In my search for information about Evans' life and work, I have had great assistance from many quarters, both within Cleobury and further afield. To all those who freely provided information, recollections, photographs and advice my thanks are due, and in particular to Doris Aldridge-Evans, Mrs M. Downes, Edwina Guest, Marilyn Howells, Jess Thompson, Miss J. Yardley, Mr John Davis, Rev. Brian Gadd, Mr F. Morrison, Mr W. Raiswell, Mr M. Ray, Mr W. Scott, Mr Ivor Simpson and Mr James Warren. The source of each photograph is shown after the caption.

---

* The main sources are listed in the Bibliography on page 21. Detailed references will be provided in an article planned for a forthcoming issue of *Cleobury Chronicles*.

List of illustrations

SECTION 1: THE LIFE OF SIMON EVANS

EARLY YEARS

Simon Evans was born on 10 August 1895 at Tynyfedu, near Llangadfan in Montgomeryshire (now Powys), the son of a Welsh hill farmer, Ellis Evans. In about 1907, Ellis and his family left the farm and moved to Birkenhead, thus enabling Simon to attend school for the first time. As a Welsh-speaking newcomer, Simon was not well accepted by his school-fellows, and mixed with them as little as possible, preferring to leave them, and the town, by escaping into the Cheshire countryside. He spent much of his time walking and swimming, and began to read under the influence of a sympathetic teacher, a young Scot, who first awakened Simon's interest in books. At the age of fourteen, he left school and started work with the Post Office. Apart from his Army service, he worked for the Post Office for the rest of his life.

At the time that war was declared on Germany in August 1914, Simon Evans was studying for a Civil Service examination, but he enlisted in the 16th Cheshires in September 1914. He was then just nineteen, but his size — he was well over 6 feet tall — and his maturity led to promotion to Sergeant before he was twenty. He was wounded more than once, and sent back to England for treatment and subsequent convalescence. In the summer of 1918, he was wounded again, and gassed. Invalided home with severely wounded legs, he successfully resisted a surgeon's proposal to amputate his right leg. He was finally discharged from the Army in May 1919, but suffered the effects of both the wounds and the gassing for the rest of his days. After discharge, he received a weekly Army pension of 18s 8d for three years.

Prematurely aged by his war experiences, he found it hard to re-establish a life back on Merseyside. He again took up work as a postman, but there was little in city life to appeal to him. His health was poor, and his weakened lungs were susceptible to attack by the polluted urban air, especially in winter. In 1926, he spent six months on the south coast in a convalescent home for ex-soldiers. He was advised to follow this by spending a few days on a walking holiday. He took the advice, and while on the holiday had the good fortune to come across a postman who wished to exchange his rural round in Cleobury Mortimer for an urban round. Evans jumped at the chance, and applied for a transfer. Although some of the doctors consulted by the Post Office thought that a lengthy rural round would be too physically demanding, Evans' determination won the day, and he moved to Cleobury towards the end of 1926.

A POSTMAN'S LIFE IN CLEOBURY

A new start in the country marked an abrupt and welcome change in Evans' fortunes. He took to Cleobury, and to his new job, with a will, responding well to the demands of his postal round. He lodged at 34 Lower Street with an old

1: In uniform (though perhaps not appreciating the hat) outside the Post Office, Lower Street. (Edwina Guest)

couple, Mr and Mrs Brighton. Mr Brighton had established himself as a leather worker and cobbler, but also took in lodgers. When, in 1935, Evans' mother and sister Kay came to Cleobury, all three of them lived together in a house (now demolished) further down Lower Street.

Those who knew him at this time frequently remark on his physical appearance. Two or three inches over six feet in height, with a powerful head, blue eyes, and reddish curly hair, he came from a family apparently known as 'The Red Giants'. Externally, at least, there seem to have been few suggestions that he was not in the best of health, although it does appear that he did not carry his postman's bag in the approved manner, as it would have put undue pressure on his chest. It is known, however, that he was not enthusiastic about wearing the Post Office uniform, and was not inclined to abide by the rules on this matter.

On a number of occasions he described, in greater or lesser detail, the essential features of his daily routine. Soon after six o'clock each morning, the mail arrived at the Post Office in Lower Street. Evans, whose lodgings were just across the street, would join his colleagues sorting the incoming mail, and before seven o'clock he would leave to start his deliveries. By way of Ron Hill, he would walk out of Cleobury up the valley of the River Rea, via the farms or hamlets of Musbatch, Nethercott, Reaside (one of several so called), Detton Hall, and Prescott Farm and Mill. As he did not need to stick to roads or footpaths, his route would have varied from day to day according to the calls he had to make. In his stretch of the river there were, he recalls, six road bridges, eight footbridges, and a number of places where the river might be crossed by means of fords or fallen trees. He would thus have had plenty of scope for planning the day's route carefully to take in the necessary visits, bearing in mind the possibilities for crossing the river. Whatever his exact route, he seemed to be heading all the time towards Abdon Burf, although the round only took him about as far north as Duddlewick Mill. This outward journey was of about twelve miles.

Somewhere near this terminal point, the Post Office had provided a rest hut. This was a normal provision for a full-time rural postman. The hut contained a stove, thus allowing the postman to dry his clothes and rest before walking back to his starting point. While in the hut, the postman could be called upon to fulfil simple Post Office duties, such as selling stamps, and accepting registered letters, licence applications and the like. Evans had to stay in his hut until three o'clock, and spent much of his time there reading or writing.

The exact location of the hut is not recorded, and the hut itself has long since been moved, but local people recall that it was on the roadside just to the east of Stottesdon Halt, a station on the Cleobury Mortimer & Ditton Priors Light Railway. Evans himself describes it as having the Rea 'not far from the doorway' and 'Hinton Wood not far distant'.

On leaving the hut, Evans would take a more direct route back to the Post Office, covering about six miles. While returning, he would announce his

2: At 'The Hut', about 1930. (Mrs M. Downes)

passage by blowing a whistle at certain points, thus giving notice that he was prepared to take letters back to the Post Office to catch the outgoing mail at 5 o'clock.

WRITER AND BROADCASTER

Evans made great use of his Post Office hut, both on and off duty. He fitted it up with bookshelves and a camp bed, and would spend weekends there, surrounded by his books in rural isolation. This may seem a little irregular but, some years later, he had no hesitation in describing his use of the hut in this way when writing for the *Post Office Magazine*. His interest in literature, first encouraged by the one sympathetic teacher he had encountered at school, flourished and he enrolled for a correspondence course in English Literature at Ruskin College, Oxford, an independent college founded in 1899 to provide education for working men. Evans' enrolment may have been made possible by the decision of the Union of Post-Office Workers in 1928 to allot two hundred guineas annually to fund correspondence courses for its members at the college. From the principal, Mr Barratt Brown, he received 'unstinted advice, encouragement and warm friendship' and he began to submit articles to, and have these accepted by, local and regional periodicals. He also began to give short talks on the wireless.

Despite his great interest in books and writing, Evans does not seem to have considered writing a book himself; the idea apparently came from elsewhere. His first book *Round About the Crooked Steeple* is dedicated to Miss Shannie Cranton 'who first drew her father's attention to my efforts on the wireless and thus inspired the publication of this volume' by Heath Cranton. As a result of his daughter's initiative, Mr Cranton maintained personal contact with Evans for many years, and came to Cleobury to visit him on several occasions.

Heath Cranton, a London-based firm, were publishers of books of country interest, many of which were collections of short pieces previously published in periodicals. *Round About the Crooked Steeple* was a book of this type, containing seventeen pieces, at least four of which had already been published in periodicals, and one, 'My Daily Round', had been broadcast 'from 2LO'. (This was the call sign for London's second transmitter, located at Alexandra Palace.) The book was published on 20 March 1931 at 3s 6d in a jacket illustrated with a rather naive view of Cleobury and its church by Ogle.* A lengthy foreword was contributed by the Reverend H. E. G. Rope, chaplain at Mawley Hall, whose own book *Forgotten England* was published by Heath Cranton later in the year. Rope and Evans developed a close friendship, which survived Rope's move to Rome in about 1938. They had a shared interest in literature, and Rope frequently lent books to Evans.

---

* I have not yet seen a jacketed copy of the first issue, but as the second printing appeared only three weeks after the first, it is unlikely that the jacket design would have been changed.

Round About the Crooked Steeple was well received, and a second printing was quickly ordered, being published on 9 April, with a third printing the following year. Amongst the many favourable reviews in the national press, the most highly valued must have been one by Vita Sackville-West in *Broadcasting*: 'Mr. Evans has not only the necessary sensitiveness to appreciate, but also the power to express in words ... To all those who love the country I recommend this book'. The final issue, in 1938, had a redrawn jacket based on Ogle's design, and Rope's foreword was entirely omitted.

The book contains a mixture of poems, anecdotes, essays and autobiographical pieces, not too long nor too weighty, just the mixture to appeal to the Arcadian taste of the 1930s. The war was slowly beginning to fade into history, and it was generally felt that armed conflict on such a scale would never be seen again. Educational reform, emancipation, the wireless, the motor-car, paid holidays, and a basic understanding of health and nutrition had all combined to liberate people from the worst excesses of industrialised urban life. The countryside was coming to be seen as a place of re-creation for townspeople, replete with traditional values, not just a place where benighted rustics dwelt, to be pitied for their lack of contact with the civilised life of towns. *Round About the Crooked Steeple* caught this new mood well.

Evans was a regular broadcaster, appearing on a variety of programmes. On some he would read one of his own stories; on others he would take part in discussions and interviews. He was certainly doing the former as early as 1930, and in 1935 he took part in one of the BBC's 'Microphone At Large' features, not dissimilar to the 'Down Your Way' programmes of our own time. Other local participants in this broadcast, made from Cleobury College (now the Old Wing of the Lacon Childe School), included Tom Worrall (a butcher), Mr Childs (a local J.P.), and the vicar of Cleobury, the Reverend Percy Malden. The programme also included a sketch based on an Evans story. A few years later he was instrumental in organising a second programme in the series, broadcast from the Wyre Forest.

FOUR MORE BOOKS

In 1932, Heath Cranton published a second book by Evans: *At Abdon Burf*, priced at 3s 6d. The jacket was designed by Hector St Luke, who had also designed the jacket for Rope's book, and was a great improvement over Ogle's work. *At Abdon Burf* was dedicated to Evans' mentor, A. Barratt Brown, the Principal of Ruskin College, Oxford.

The contents are, broadly, of the same mix as before, with one interesting exception. The first piece, entitled 'At Abdon Burf', comprises five sections, which together form a short and powerful story. Even though this only totals 34 pages, it is by far the longest piece in any of Evans' books except *Applegarth*, and suggests that he was exploring ways of escaping from the limitations of the five-minute radio talk or the short newspaper article.

Two years later, the Midland News Association published a collection of articles under the title *Midland Leaves*. These had originally been contributed to *The Express & Star*, a West Midlands evening newspaper, by Wilfred Byford-Jones writing as 'Quaestor'. For three of his articles, Byford-Jones must have teamed up with Simon Evans, for they all have local settings. The first of these describes some local characters, the second tells of an outing of the Cleobury Mortimer Fire Brigade, and the third, 'Walking Post Offices', gives us a familiar description of the working day of a rural postman in the Cleobury area. Byford-Jones accompanied one such postman on his round. Despite the postman's being called 'Burns' in the article, it is quite clearly Evans who took Byford-Jones out on his round. He even gives a description of the hut 'fitted with a desk, books, a seat, an oil stove and a small window. In a rack was a churchwarden's pipe from Broseley.'

In 1935 came Evans' third book: *More Tales from Round About the Crooked Steeple*, priced at 3s 6d. This is another collection of articles, anecdotes and essays, dedicated to his niece Diana, and has a fine pictorial jacket by Hector St Luke showing Cleobury's main street, and a frontispiece depicting the Talbot Hotel and the steeple. The author's acknowledgement shows that much of his effort was still being put into writing articles for regional and national periodicals. Nearly half the book is composed of character sketches — all of well-known and recognisable people, described under their own names, e.g. Tom Worrall and 'Slackrope' Williams, and also three of those chosen by Byford-Jones: Nipper Cooke, Will Link, and Soldier George. It must not be assumed that because Byford-Jones' book appeared before Evans' book, the latter had derived any ideas from the former. In fact the obvious co-operation between the two authors makes the reverse more likely to be true. In any case, most, if not all, of the items had already been published in newspapers before the books came out.

Despite the generally light-hearted tone of *More Tales*, it contains a positive reminder that Evans' health was still giving him trouble as 'the wounds and hurts I received during the Great War are still the drag-anchor of my life'. One of the articles describes the three months Evans spent in Birmingham General Hospital in the early months of 1933. Even in hospital, he was an impressive and striking figure, and his stay is still remembered today by one of the young nurses who cared for him. She describes him as 'an exceptionally handsome and charming man', popular with all the nurses. She can even recall the type of pyjamas he wore, a small but convincing demonstration of how unusual and memorable a man he was.

Not surprisingly, Evans wished to experiment with a full-length novel, and Cranton published his *Applegarth* in 1936. In brief, this describes a phase in the life of Roger, the youngest son of a south Shropshire farmer, the domineering Rolf Roderick. We follow the fortunes of father and son for some years, until Rolf's death allows Roger, rather than either of his brothers, to take on the tenancy of the farm. Almost for the first time the author tackles the passions and tensions engendered by family relationships, and gives his tale a continuous, if uneven, plot. The ending is such that a sequel could naturally follow; Evans certainly considered this at one time.

Although the novel form allowed Evans a broad canvas for the first time, the elements and settings of the story all arise out of his own personal experience. Applegarth, the farm, is unashamedly placed in south Shropshire. When Roger leaves home, it is to the army and to Liverpool that he goes, both important segments of Evans' own life. It is, however, south Shropshire which dominates, with long accounts of events in Cleobury, including a comic interlude featuring the Cleobury Fire Brigade, observed by Lofty Reardon, the postman.

Finally, in 1938, came Evans' last book: *Shropshire Days and Shropshire Ways*, again priced at 3s 6d. The similarity of this to other Cranton titles suggests that it was the publisher's choice, not the author's. The jacket was again by St Luke, but six uninspiring line drawings by Alan Dakin are included within the text. Although similar in style to Evans' previous collections, it includes some useful autobiographical pieces. 'Up the Valley' is a description of his postal round, but the adoption by the Post Office of motorcycles to serve rural areas led to his being taken off this round in 1935. His disaffection with this turn of events is shown in 'Farewell to the Valley'. Evans was then required to ride a motorcycle, but he found this not at all to his taste. He describes it as a 'horrible machine' and a 'hideous contraption' whose care took up too much of his time, leaving too little for writing. He was later given another walking round to the south of Cleobury, taking in Neen Sollars, as he describes in 'Fresh Woods and Pastures New'.

MARRIAGE

Far more important than the change of round was Evans' meeting with Doris Aldridge in 1937. This is described, in veiled terms, in 'In Praise of Brogues', one of the pieces in *Shropshire Days*. As might be expected of a man in whose life walking was so significant, Evans attached great importance to his choice of shoes. After singing the praises of a particular pair of 'bonny, well-proportioned brogues' which had cost him a whole week's pay,* he recounts the results of having worn them when taking part in a country entertainment programme on the wireless. He had subsequently received a letter from a fellow performer:

DEAR MR. EVANS, — Please forgive me for writing to you, and for the — er — personal question I'm going to ask. Are you really a postman?

By the way, I'm the female who sang before you gave your talk.

You see, while going home with my friends you caused an argument. They said you were a postman! I said you couldn't be because your brogues must have cost at least three guineas. I said you were a fictitious kind of postman; I think you must be a farmer . . .

---

* Having started at a weekly wage of 17s, Evans had progressed to 58s by 1937.

3: Doris Aldridge, about 1935. (Doris Aldridge-Evans)

4: *The Ron Hill house under construction, 1938. (Doris Aldridge-Evans)*

5: *At Ron Hill, 1938. Simon and Doris at left, Harry (holding David) at right.*
(Doris Aldridge-Evans)

The writer was Doris Aldridge, 'Aunty Doris', a young singer and broadcaster working full-time for the BBC, who obviously had a good eye for the price of shoes! Her letter led to the development of a close relationship, resulting in marriage to Simon on 11 October 1938. Fittingly, *Shropshire Days* is dedicated 'To Doris Aldridge and to the memory of a most excellent pair of brogues'.

Doris recalls their wedding day with great gusto. It was largely unplanned, and decidedly informal. A friend was sent with a motorcycle combination to fetch Doris from the Oxfordshire village where she lived, and take her to meet Simon in Birmingham, where he had hired a car. A close friend, Sam Price, was asked by phone if he'd care to be best man, and he agreed, so the party made for Bridgnorth, where the wedding took place in the Registry Office, by special licence. Sam then offered a wedding breakfast at Tenbury Wells, so Simon drove to The Swan. After this, Simon decided the couple should go to Wales for a honeymoon. Off to Dolgellau they went, only to meet with cold disapproval in the town's leading hotel, as they lacked both the luggage and the demeanour expected of a married couple. A frantic shopping expedition in the local emporium produced a tiny suitcase, and pyjamas and toothbrushes for both. Armed with these, they left Dolgellau and made for Aberystwyth where Simon knew a lady who owned a seaside hotel. After a hair-raising drive in the dark through the Welsh mountains they arrived safely at Aberystwyth, and could finally relax.

6: Doris, Judy, Simon and colleagues, 9 March 1940. (Mr F. Morrison)

The Evans settled in Cleobury, buying a plot of land and having a substantial house built for them on Ron Hill to a design by Doris. Alas, Simon's health was still poor, and despite writing in late 1938 'I am fit and well', within a year he had to give up work as a postman. He died in the Queen Elizabeth Hospital, Birmingham, on 9 August 1940, the day before his forty-fifth birthday. The cause of his death was, in essence, tuberculosis, brought on by the severe gas damage he had suffered in 1918. His ashes were scattered on Abdon Burf, for so long the distant beacon of his daily walks.

His fame was probably at its greatest in the late 1930s when his broadcasts would have brought his name (and that of Cleobury) to the attention of many thousands, but he is by no means forgotten in South Shropshire, the land which gave him fourteen years of fulfilment.

THE LAST FIFTY YEARS

Although it is now over fifty years since Evans' death, he is well remembered, and with affection, in Cleobury and the surrounding area. Many of his characters are still talked of, particularly men like Nipper Cooke and Will Link, for our modern times do not seem to produce men of such individuality. It is even rare these days for a man to be widely known by a nickname, yet nicknames abound in Evans' tales — Nipper Cooke, Old Dig, Soldier George, Slackrope Williams — and this surely reflects the practice of the day.

Evans has been the subject of frequent newspaper articles, most of which have added little to our knowledge of the man and his work; however, their very publication is evidence of a continuing interest in Evans, and his romantic life story. His books have long since been out of print and difficult to obtain, but in 1978 a local bookseller and publisher, Kenneth Tomkinson, published an anthology of Evans' work. The success of the anthology, which was twice reprinted, shows the appeal still exercised by Evans.

There have been other memorials; a new cul-de-sac beyond New Inn Row has been named Simon Evans Close, with an appropriate bronze plaque affixed below the street sign, and an inscribed brass plate was displayed in the Post Office (albeit temporarily removed). In 1984, Cleobury Players staged a highly successful dramatisation by Jim Bartlett of some of Evans' stories as a part of the Cleobury Mortimer & District Midsummer Scene.

For many years, and on many occasions, suggestions have come from various quarters, including the Parish Council, that Evans' life and work should be commemorated by dedicating a footpath between Cleobury and Stottesdon as a 'Simon Evans Way'. One idea was to use part of the trackbed of the light railway, which was closed in 1965. To date, nothing has been done. Apart from the resources required, there is the very real problem that his route was not fixed, and often departed from rights of way. Therefore, either new rights of way would be required, which would be difficult to secure, or, if a route along existing rights of way were chosen, it might carry the name, but would not in fact be Evans' actual path.

In 1976, a local photographer working for the *Kidderminster Shuttle*, George Munday, was inspired by Evans' writing to produce a series of photographs depicting the landscapes, buildings, scenes and sights which Evans would have seen on his daily round. At the suggestion of David Gaukroger, a Cleobury resident, and with the assistance of the Arts Council, an exhibition of these photographs was mounted in Ludlow as part of the 1976 Ludlow Festival. It was later transferred to Stourport, and to other local venues. Unfortunately this collection of evocative studies has now been dispersed, although there is no reason why another generation of photographers could not be given the opportunity to make their own record and interpretation of 'Evans country'.

EVANS AS A WRITER
Although often expressing a great love of literature, and rejoicing in the companionship of books, Evans also made clear his greater love for the company of his fellow men. In 1938, having written five books, he still maintained:*

> I do not wish it to be understood that the reading of books and writing have the first or all-important place in my way of living. Life, I think, is not to study but to live. While I have health and strength let me walk among my fellow men. I would rather meet my farmer friends than sit and dream. I pray that no dreams or hobbies of mine will ever rob me of life itself, of my meetings with men at work in the fields and in the market-place; nor do I wish to lose the pleasure which is mine when I join a game of bowls on the village green, or when I am one of a company who exchange good-humoured banter and chaff.

On more than one occasion, when contrasting life in Cleobury to that in Birkenhead, Evans remarks, paradoxically, that in this sparsely populated corner of Shropshire he came to know perhaps a thousand people, whereas in the town this would only have been a few dozen. Conversely, he laments the lack of bookish friends; 'among the country people who became my friends I found no book lovers'. As we have seen, he did have the friendship of the literary Father Rope, but this was perhaps not enough.

So, literature was not the most important part of Evans' life; yet it is difficult to say what did take pride of place. It was not religion, despite his repeated vision of the Hand of God reaching down from the skies, and his declared admiration for his god-fearing Regimental Sergeant Major. When in 1935, Rope took Evans to task for his lack of 'a consistent philosophy of life' and (in effect) a lack of religious conviction, Evans made some effort to explain his views at length. He could not accept that a Church which professed clear ethical and moral values

---

* The Way By Which I Have Come'. *The Countryman* Oct 1938. The complete article may be found on pages 25–29.

should have become so involved with the military machine of the Great War, yet show no signs, nearly twenty years later, of wishing to distance itself from the armed services. Neither religion nor family life, nor sport, nor indeed the job of being a postman, seems to have been pre-eminent. Yet if good company were all, as the above passage implies, why did Evans spend so much time and effort on his literary endeavours, both written and broadcast?

He would have been less than human if he had not derived some pleasure, some satisfaction, both from the fame and the fortune that being a writer brought. As a broadcaster, he would have been quite well known in the West Midlands, even if not a household name. The continuing acceptance of his work by editors and producers must have been gratifying, and he would surely have taken pride in the growing list of his books. Marriage did not curtail this, for in the twenty-two months between his marriage and his death, at least five of his articles were published, and a sixth appeared in 1941. At this time, he was also working on another book, and made at least one broadcast.

His success as a writer rests more on craftsmanship than on creativity. Here is no mighty imaginative genius, but a man whose deep love of the countryside, seasonal colour, honest toil and good company, provided him with a ready source of material. Accepted into a rural community, Evans enjoyed the sense of belonging, and used the insights provided by this acceptance to examine and record the ways of country people. Almost always he takes the part of the countryman and, in *More Tales*, he defends his own choice of being a postman:

> It seems a dull and poor end for a man who might have done better, for a man who — maybe — had great ideas and hopes. Still, it's not as dull as you may think; life is full of compensations . . . So, Harry my friend, I'm just a country postman — what of it? My daily round is a round of pleasure, life is not what people call it. If your eyes are quick to see and your ears quick in hearing, and if you believe in your heart that
>
> > *Nature never did betray*
> > *The heart that loved her,*
>
> then you'll live a life all your own, and you'll laugh quietly at public opinion and intellectuals.

His appreciation of the countryside is on a very human level; he is by no means a writer on natural history. Detailed observations of natural phenomena are largely absent; he is more concerned with the effects of weather and seasons upon the humans who inhabit the countryside. When he identifies the birds, flowers or trees which he observes, it is more to set the scene than to display or impart knowledge. He is moved by the spiritual values of the countryside, in the way that Hugh Massingham and Tom Rolt were, not by pursuit of biological or ecological understanding. Despite a desire to walk alone, his feeling for the countryside is very much a human one, and the market place, the inn and the postal round are for him part of the web of country experience.

On at least two occasions, he lists authors whose books he chose to have to hand, so it is likely that to some extent their writing influenced his own. The first list comprises Jefferies, Hudson, Keats, Shelley, Herrick, Gray, Davies, de la Mare, Blunden, Sassoon, Graves, Owen, Masefield, Belloc, Borrow, Housman, Sackville-West and Carlyle. The second, compiled at much the same time but for publication in a less literary periodical, is made up of Borrow, Belloc, Burns, Carlyle, Aurelius, Kipling, Masefield, Mary Webb, Lamb, Hazlitt, Hardy, Stevenson, E. V. Lucas, Carpenter, Jefferies and Hudson.* In his own writing, he rarely has need to discuss any book or author at length, but he does make more than one mention of Ruskin and of Mary Webb, and includes an essay on Carlyle and Emerson in *At Abdon Burf.*

His writing depends largely on his own experiences. Although this must be true for many writers, it is more transparent in his case than is usual. There is, in his work, little of the purely imaginative; almost all the settings and episodes are clearly parallels of events or periods in his own life. The sources of his inspiration are, indeed, even more limited than this might suggest for he relies little on his life before coming to Cleobury. His early life in Wales, his youth and manhood on Merseyside, and his years in the Army make a disproportionately small contribution to his writing.

Doubtless his war service would have provided material for many articles, indeed for whole books. In the 1920s and 1930s, however, the subject was already well worn, and Evans presumably chose not to add his recollections to the flood of words about the war. Nevertheless, there were two themes which moved him deeply, and to which he returned more than once. The first was the inspiration he drew from his Regimental Sergeant Major, 'a perfect soldier' who 'moved a thousand men with greater ease than the N.C.O.s moved ten'. 'Occasionally he would begin his work with the battalion with these words, each one fired as if from a rifle, "Upright in body, upright in mind, and fear no man on God's earth." These words have helped me more than creeds and philosophies.'**

The other powerful memory of his war years was the killing of a young Prussian soldier, followed by the stark and painful realisation that there lay the body of a man like himself, who would not now return to his home and loved ones. Evans recalls this several times, once with some force in one of his more moving poems 'Memories', which describes the moment when he searches for the identity disc from the neck of the Prussian, and finds instead a locket containing a picture of a young woman:

---

* See pages 28 and 31 for the original contexts.
** See, for instance, '1930 — What of Life?' in *More Tales,* and his *Countryman* article on pages 25 to 29.

The portrait in my bloodied hand
Was —— his chosen of the land.
And as I gazed, 'twas then I saw
The cursed horror of the war.
In distant homes are broken hearts
Because we puppets play our parts.

He has, to modern tastes, a few faults. There is a tendency towards repetition of both theme and words. The former arises, perhaps, from working with a limited stock of material, largely his own experience of a bachelor life in south Shropshire. It may be because most of his writing is of short articles that he is inclined to fall back on the same adjectives again and again. For example, countrymen's hands are frequently described as 'mahogany coloured' and woodpeckers always seem to be 'green-backed'. Homer, it is true, uses the repeated epithet as a deliberate technique; maybe Evans did too, and the result only jars a little nowadays because we can read the collected articles in book form.

Perhaps more serious is his occasional yielding to the temptation to display countrymen as bucolic bumpkins, particularly when they venture from their familiar country settings to taste and tangle with the marvels of modern city life. Such a patronising attitude, it seems, caused some resentment during his lifetime, and today's readers still find that it mars some of his work.

Strength he has, undoubtedly. His evocation of country life is enjoyable. He captures well the wit and wisdom of the farmer and the shop-keeper, the publican and the poacher. He can tell a good tale, and hold his reader's interest. His dedication to walking through the countryside, merely observing and appreciating the sights this offers, is inspirational. To read Evans is to long for the winding lane, the rolling hillside, the buffeting of the wind, a glimpse of pheasant or rabbit, and good company at a pub fireside at the end of the day.

BIBLIOGRAPHY

Works by Simon Evans:

Round About the Crooked Steeple: a Shropshire harvest. London: Heath Cranton, 1931. First published 20 March 1931; 2nd imp 9 April 1931; 3rd imp 15 Nov 1932; 4th imp 31 Jan 1938.

At Abdon Burf: more tales from Shropshire. London: Heath Cranton, 1932.

More Tales From Round About the Crooked Steeple. London: Heath Cranton. 1935.

Applegarth: a novel. London: Heath Cranton, 1936.

Shropshire Days and Shropshire Ways. London: Heath Cranton, 1938.

The Way by Which I Have Come. *The Countryman.* Vol 18(1). Oct 1938. pp84-93.

A Simon Evans Anthology. Kidderminster: Tomkinson, 1978. Originally issued as a limited (but not numbered) edition of 150, this was reprinted in 1979 and 1981.

Evans is also known to have contributed to the following periodicals:

The Birmingham Mail
The Bookmark
The Christian Science Monitor
Country Life
The Countryman
The Daily Herald
The Leeds Mercury
The Liverpool Weekly Post
The Nottingham Guardian
The Post Office Magazine
The Wellington Journal & Shrewsbury News

SECTION TWO

This section contains items written by Evans, which have been published but not previously collected into book form. Although much of Evans' published work has some auto-biographical content, the first few items in this section are especially interesting as they provide more personal information than is normally found in Evans' writings.

TWO LETTERS
(from *Cleobury Chronicles* Vol 1 1991)

Evans' only full-length novel, *Applegarth*, is obviously set in south Shropshire, but with some of the names of places (and people) changed. It is, therefore, interesting to read the author's comments on his book in the following letters.

Cleobury Mortimer 9 — August — 1936

My dear Friends

My mother wishes me to thank you and I also wish to thank you for your letter of congratulation and good wishes.

I was sorry to hear that your holiday plans were upset — you certainly made the best of what you had.

In Wales I had very fair weather — only one morning was I forced to stay indoors and then not more than an hour or so. I saw the Welsh Coast as far South as Tenby and a good deal of the rugged north and middle parts. I spent half a day in the National Library of Wales — now half furnished and partly filled. It will be a grand place in a year or so when, I understand, everything will be in order.

Regarding my novel, I thought "Applegarth" would be a better title than "Roger Roderick" over which I pondered for a while. I have no need to say that the background will be — for the most part — the Clee Hills and the Rea Valley — a little Dale running from the Rea towards Titterstone I have called Garthdale.

I feel that my treatment of the action and the life — low life, a good deal of it — will not please many people who wrote to me about my early tales and essays. The life of the ordinary people in the country — I mean working farmers and their families and the folk with whom they rub shoulders — is not one long sweet song and I have tried to give a fair picture of it. However, crude as some of the life is and hard as some of the men and women live — even today — I have, I hope, drawn a picture which shows many sorts and conditions of South Shropshire natives — some of them are rough and I hope the readers will see what I have seen in the roughest of them — some threads of goodness — some milk of human kindness. My picture may be unpleasant in parts — but what is life for many men and women? Well — I must wait for the opinions of readers and critics.

By the way — later on — if you should have somewhere on the shelf at the Library a novel — "The Heyday in the Blood" by Geraint Goodwin — a Montgomeryshire man — I would be pleased if you could put it in the Cleobury Box. I believe the book deals with country and people not far from Chirbury — I've read some very good reviews of this work — probably you have heard about it. I'm in no hurry for it — but some day I would like to read it.

We all — here — send our kind regards & good wishes to you all.

Yours sincerely, Simon

Cleobury Mortimer
17. Nov. 1936

Dear Percy

Many thanks for your letter and all your very kind words about "Applegarth".
I am glad the reading of it gave you some pleasure — it is rather a rough story
— in parts — but actual life is still more rough and I did want to give a picture
of life as the ordinary man lives it. I'm glad "Country Life" saw that point —
maybe you saw their review — they said —"most novelists have no choice but
to deal with the folk of village, farm, market and inn — as observers; Mr Evans
is one of themselves and this fact gives a pervading reality to his tale — etc etc
— in his study of Roger Roderick and his farmer father he has drawn two men
who, whether for good or ill, are of the very stuff of England".

Forgive me if you have already seen "Country Life's" review. The Times Lit.
Sup. — Morning Post — and many others say nice things about my effort, and,
like you, many of them ask about a sequel. Well, a sequel is somewhere, very far
back, in my mind at present. If I had my old walking round I would be able to
give it more thought and, probably, feel more like tackling it. However, like
"Applegarth", when the time is right and the story ripe — it will fight its way out
— whether for good or ill — as Country Life say.

Many thanks indeed for G. Goodwin's book "The Heyday in Blood". It is
a tale of the country of my birth — a well written piece of work — if you have
not read it you must put it on your list.

Oh, by the way, in a recent letter you had a few shots at naming the important
places in "Applegarth". Noctorum Common you have right — but the other
places — real enough — have been imported so that "placing" them is difficult.
For instance "The Seven Stars" is in the Wyre Forest where, of course, it has
another name. I had to be careful with Applegarth —Shepherdine — and the
Seven Stars — as I did not wish any local people to claim that they had been
drawn on. There may be slight traces — perhaps fairly strong traces to close
observers living about here — of actual people in some of my characters. I can
quite imagine that the hero — and I'm fairly certain that the heroine — of a novel
would object to — well — to all their interests and movements — and thoughts,
and so on, being outlined for all the people of their neighbourhood to read —
while they — the heros and heroines, I mean — were living their lives in the same
place. That's rather mixed up but I think you see my point. One very nice girl,
on my old round, has already threatened what she will do if I write one word
about her — it's too terrible to contemplate! Mother — Kay and I send our
kindest regards to all at St Mawes and Glanavon.

Yours aye, Simon

THE WAY BY WHICH I HAVE COME
(from *The Countryman* October 1938)

Many of our readers must have come across the country books of Simon Evans, postman, or heard him over the Wireless. When his fine figure appeared at Idbury lately we were impressed by the strength of his personality and by his gallant and kindly fronting of life. Authorship and broadcasting have not stopped his labours as a postman, though sometimes he has had to get a substitute for a day. Because of War injuries to his head and chest the authorities allow him to dispense with the regulation cap and carry his postman's bag in his own way. Among his books are 'Round about the Crooked Steeple', 'More Tales' and 'Shropshire Days and Shropshire Ways'.

I spent my early childhood in the heart of the Welsh mountains, my schooldays and telegraph messenger days amid the rush and roar which are part of the life of a seaport.

My schooldays on the Merseyside were not happy. I spoke a curious mixture of Welsh and English, and fights with boys who ridiculed my speech were frequent. Apart from these almost daily battles, all I remember of my few years at school is a young Scots teacher, whose pleasure it was to sit and read to her class, whenever she had an opportunity, extracts from 'Treasure Island', and 'Coral Island' and the tales of the Round Table.

Because of my strong Welsh accent I felt myself to be a foreigner in that crowded city, and it was my joy to escape whenever I could to the Cheshire countryside. I would not join with other boys in their games. Swimming and walking were my recreations. I began to read a little and became something of a dreamer.

While still a youth I joined the Army. The War years brought what seemed to be the end of my life. Wounded, gassed and aged by experiences I cannot forget, I returned to the Merseyside. The beliefs and enthusiasms of my boyhood were no more. The soul-destroying War had poisoned my body and mind. My health and strength, which I had accepted as a right and of which I had been so proud, seemed lost for ever. The dreams of my boyhood were ashes and mould. How I envied my cousins who had remained among the hills of Wales with their sheep.

I made many friends during my Army days. Looking back at those years I feel now that I was far too serious. I was little more than a boy, but my height and perhaps my serious outlook brought me early promotion. Very soon I was a sergeant. Twice I made attempts to get back into the ranks, but I was told to obey orders. While in my teens I was in charge of fifty or sixty men, and I performed duties which, when I think of them now, leave me amazed and puzzled.

One man I met during my Army life stands out above all others, the regimental sergeant-major of the Coldstreams. In appearance he was the finest man I have ever seen, the picture of health and a perfect soldier. He never used strong language, but at his word the battalion moved as one man. It seemed to me that he moved a thousand men with greater ease than the N.C.O.s moved ten. Even now my back stiffens when I think of his early morning parades. He stood far off and his words came like shots — 'Upright in Body, upright in Mind, and fear no man on God's earth'. Out of his hearing, we called him 'Dai Left'. His left leg, although it seemed sound enough as he moved about, had been smashed, and he sometimes roared, 'If my left leg was right, I'd show you'.

However, at the end of the War my legs were smashed and my lungs were scarred. I left the Army with a pension of 18s. 8d. per week and a good deal of hospital treatment facing me. After three years my pension was stopped. I was a town postman and I looked a better man than I really was. Right up to 1926 I had long periods of hospital life. Old wounds broke open and refused to heal, the fogs of the Mersey damaged still more my already weakened lungs.

In those years of ill-health and disappointments, like many another I brooded over my troubles. No one asked why I was silent or why I walked alone. I often asked myself these questions, but I could not or dared not answer. In an effort to forget I turned to books. I read all kinds. (Why, I wonder, are the libraries of hospitals and convalescent homes stored with so much trash?) Most of the books I read were of no value, but some were good. The seed sowed by that Scots teacher began to grow. A passage in Emerson's 'Compensation' had a remarkable effect on me: 'Has a man a defect of temper that unfits him to live in society? Thereby he is driven to entertain himself alone, and acquire habits of self-help; and thus, like the wounded oyster, he mends his shell with pearl.' I was unfit to live in society, and these words became a kind of motto for my life. The wounds and hurts I received in the War have been my drag-anchor, but the compensations I have found have been great.

All my holidays, in any freedom which came to me, I spent walking in the country. Any part of England unknown to me was a foreign country. The satisfaction I found in wandering about, weak though I was, soothed my mind. My walking holidays were, and still are, the great pleasures of my life. Never a ridge of hills but I must know what lies beyond; a hamlet in a leafy dale fills me with a glad sense of expectation; a lane staggering up a hillside, over heath and heather, and on into a wood which clothes the shoulder of some distant height, may lead me into a fairyland -

> By hanging woods and hamlets
>   That gaze through orchards down
> On many an windmill turning
>   And far-discovered town.

I remember early one morning, many years ago, walking on the Longmynd. A deep feeling of wonder, almost of fear, clutched me as I stood to watch a dawn full of indescribable glory.

In 1926 I realized that I must start again, build, out of the ruins of youth, a new life. I made up my mind to break away from the town and begin afresh. I know now that, in spite of the years I spent in town, I have always been at heart a countryman. When, after several months in a convalescent home on the south coast I returned to the town, I was more determined than ever that I would not stay there. I felt drawn towards the Land of my Fathers, but it seemed to me that the mountains of Wales were too cold and grim, and I had seen too much of the cold, grim side of life. Chance sent me to a warmer richer countryside, the country of the Clees, not far distant from

> valleys of springs and rivers
> By Ony and Teme and Clun,
> The country for easy livers,
> The quietest under the sun.

I spent the few days' leave due to me walking in the Welsh Border country. While in South Shropshire I met a rural postman who wished to live in the town. I decided that if it were possible I would exchange with him. A few days later I sent my application forward. Doctors disagreed. Some said I would never be able to walk eighteen miles of hill and dale every day in all sorts of wind and weather. 'Well', I said, 'if I must die I'd rather die on some hill-top breathing good clean air than die in any long, unlovely street of your town'. One doctor, Hal Leete, now in Yorkshire, was my very good friend, and was strongly in favour of South Shropshire. In this way I became a rural postman and walked the valley of the Rea.

For some months I found my daily walk a stiff task. It was winter time when I began, and that winter was a bad one. However, I lived quietly, rested as often as I could, and after a while the life became a pleasure. My daily walk was a daily pilgrimage; as I grew stronger I felt that I was escaping from the prison my life had been, back to the sun and air I loved, back to a freedom and a quiet happiness which I longed for.

At the limit of my outward walk I had a shelter hut, a little place supplied by the Post Office in which a man could rest in fair comfort until the hour arrived when he was due to start on his return walk. This hut had a good deal to do with my return to fair health and strength. The river Rea flowed not far from the doorway, and from the open window I could see the high-reared head of Titterstone Clee, 1752 feet above sea-level. Titterstone is a brave, bold hill, with windswept heights and a clean line against the sky. It has a look of rugged strength. Across the Wheatland Vale, a little to the north but nearer than Titterstone, stood Brown Clee Hill, whale-backed and richly wooded. I always think of these two hills as twins — brother and sister. Titterstone, grim and strong, defies every storm. In a way I cannot understand he somehow adds to my own strength, to my endurance and patience. There is, about a wide sky and high hills, something which soothes my mind. When I walk among the hills I find that calmness which is the great good. The Brown Clee, in contrast with Titterstone, is well wooded, warm and tenderly beautiful, 'Her ways are ways of pleasantness and all her paths are peace.'

Set in such surroundings — the stream a few yards away, Hinton Wood not far distant, and, within easy reach, the farm of a man who proved to be my very good friend — I gained a quiet happiness.

My predecessor in the hut had been, during his off-duty hours, something of a gardener, a cobbler and a saddle and harness doctor. After a while I changed the appearance of this little room of my own. I spent short week-ends there. I swept, scrubbed and cleaned. I built a camp bed along the back wall and nailed up a couple of bookshelves. A briar pipe or two and a long Broseley church-warden hung from a home-made pipe-rack. A jar of tobacco stood half-hidden in a handful of cool leaves which I picked, almost every morning, from the riverside.

When my little library began to grow I knew my body and mind were growing stronger. How much do I not owe to books?

> What are my books? My friends, my loves,
> My church, my tavern and my only wealth.

I began to collect books, 'the true university in these days', but among the country people who became my friends I found no book lovers. I set about looking for a guide. I wrote to Ruskin College, Oxford, asking if I might take a correspondence course in English Literature. The work I sent in at the end of each month — essays on country subjects, character sketches and poems — attracted the attention of the principal. We exchanged long letters, and it was arranged for me to make the course almost what I wished it to be. From Mr. Barratt Brown I received unstinted advice, encouragement and warm friendship; I have never been able to thank him as I wish I could.

I became a reader and amateur writer. One or other of my books accompanied me wherever I went till it became tattered. What a goodly company of books I have gathered together — Jefferies, Hudson, Keats, Shelley, Herrick, Gray, Davies, de la Mare, Blunden, Sassoon, Graves, Owen, Masefield, Belloc, Borrow, Housman, Sackville West, Carlyle.

The first book I wrote was published as a result of a Wireless talk I gave from the old Savoy Hill station. A publisher heard the talk and made a journey to Shropshire to see me. He took away with him what appeared as 'Round About the Crooked Steeple'. Since then I have written a great deal about the Shropshire countryside and Shropshire people. On the slopes of Clee Hills and in the valley of the Rea I feel sure I know more than a thousand people and know them well — in the town I never knew more than ten or a dozen.

But now that I am fit and well I do not wish it to be understood that the reading of books and writing have the first or all-important place in my way of living. Life, I think, is not to study but to live. While I have health and strength let me walk among my fellow men. I would rather meet my farmer friends than sit and dream. I pray that no dreams or hobbies of mine will ever rob me of life itself, of my meetings with men at work in the fields and in the market-place; nor do I wish to lose the pleasure which is mine when I join in a game of bowls on the village green, or when I am one of a company who exchange good-humoured banter and chaff. Countrymen have wit and wisdom in plenty. If we live among them, work and play with them, we can touch with grace the common pattern of our lives.

MY LITTLE PLACE IN THE COUNTRY
(from *The Post Office Magazine* January 1939)

A dozen or so years ago a town postman lived in one of those houses, in a long, long row of houses, not more than a mile from one of England's largest shipyards. Almost all his days, certainly all his working days, were spent in that maze we call a town — bricks and mortar in seemingly endless rows, tracks and 'bus routes where endless streams of traffic moved; and tube trains ran underground with a roar like thunder.

How did it come about that this postman suddenly became the owner — or rather an occupier who paid neither rent nor rates — of a little place in the country?

This little place had what house agents call "an excellent southern aspect and extensive views." The occupier also had the right to wander over tens of thousands of acres of glorious countryside. The old rhyme says —

> "Happy is the eye
> 'Twixt Severn and Wye,
> But thrice happy he,
> 'Twixt Severn and Clee."

And certainly the countryside between Severn and Clee is wonderful, particularly the long winding Valley of the Rea.

From the door of this little place in the country one could see "the everlasting hills" — the rich, well-wooded slopes of Brown Clee, Shropshire's highest hill, 1,792 feet above sea level, and Titterstone Clee, bold rugged, wind-swept, 1,750 feet high. The Rea, a winding silver stream, ran down the valley only a few yards from the fence. Rich pastoral land stretched away from both banks of the river to distant common land and woodland.

And the little place in the country sheltered by the hills, and surrounded by all the beauty of an unspoiled English landscape, is — or was — a rural postman's shelter hut.

I am the postman who lived in the town. I have always been at heart a countryman and so I became a rural postman and the lucky occupier of this little place in the country. For many years it was my study until, at last, a revision of duties swept it away. Now I often think of what I could see from the window of that hut — all those things which are, I think, the warp and woof of our lives; the hills, the woods, the fields, the green hollows where the waters of streams and brooks ran babbling and chuckling to the river, the cattle and the corn, the stables and shippons of a nearby farm, and, now and then, one of the slow-moving men, a waggoner or shepherd, crossing a distant meadow. Occasionally in a lane near the hut I met one of these old men, Woodhouse his name was, he always brought to my mind Walter de la Mare's words -

> "Softly along the road of evening,
>   In a twilight dim with rose,
> Wrinkled with age and drenched with dew
>   Old Nod, the shepherd, goes."

They are not clever, these quiet countrymen, but they are wise with wisdom they have inherited from their fathers; hard working and patient they are, too, for they know that the good things of this life are made slowly.

And so that little hut in the heart of rural England, with sometimes the scent of wet soil, sometimes the tang of upland air about it, became my den — a room of my own. I swept and scrubbed it. I built a camp-bed for myself and nailed shelves all about the walls, then I began to gather round me all those books, all those friends I had longed for. A strange company they were — George Borrow and Hilaire Belloc, Bobbie Burns and Thomas Carlyle, Marcus Aurelius, and Kipling, Masefield and Mary Webb, Lamb and Hazlitt, Hardy, R.L.S. and E.V. Lucas, Edward Carpenter, Richard Jefferies and W.H. Hudson; all these and many more became my friends, ready to entertain me whenever I wished. I see them yet on those stout plain shelves of mine —

> "They stood together, row on row,
> The men who sang for singing's sake."

How lucky I was, I had all the best thoughts of scores of wise men, and these thoughts were written in their best, carefully chosen English, made plain for me to understand.

And now, alas, that little place in the country is no more. Truth to tell it was not a gem of architecture. I do not think any village carpenter I know would point to it and say — "Look at my work. I am proud of it." But it was wind-proof and rain-proof. I made it a comfortable place and it stored a good number of my books, and books can mean so much to a man. How do men live without them, I wonder. No — the hut had neither beauty nor romance, but it was the first room of my own I ever had, and with my books, with pen and paper, I spent many happy hours there.

Some few booklovers called to see me; how true it is that "a fellow-feeling makes one wondrous kind." A farm lad who wrote verses in his spare time came now and then, and a schoolmaster from the North often called — he is still my good friend. A parson, who lived a lonely life in a Clee Hill village, called to sit and talk for hours, and a plump old man with a cherubic smile would call; he always arrived in a fast sports car and because of his mild manners and quiet ways I often thought he was a bishop playing truant. He had travelled all over the world, he was a scholar, a philosopher, and most excellent company.

The countryside in that long valley is, I think, the most glorious in all England. I cannot forget it. When I have a day of freedom I go that way to enjoy all the scents, all the sights and sounds I know so well.

31

7–9: Three photographs, taken in late 1930 by Norman Thompson Williams, for possible use by Heath Cranton, publishers of Evans' books. (Marilyn Howells)

We have, many of us, a love for the good things of the past, we are apt to cling to those things which have brought us happiness. My little place in the country was my happy retreat, and stored within it were so many of my friends — my books.

> "What are my books? My friends, my loves,
> My church, my tavern, and my only wealth."

(It was in his "little place in the country" that Simon Evans wrote his books that deal with the warm-hearted folk that live in the Rea Valley and on the slopes of Titterstone and Brown Clee Hill. Many requests have been received for the titles of these books. Here they are. *Shropshire Days and Shropshire Ways, Round About the Crooked Steeple, At Abdon Burf* and *More Tales from Round About the Crooked Steeple*. Almost the whole of his novel, *Applegarth*, is set in the same Shropshire countryside.)

PAST AND PRESENT
(from *The Post Office Magazine* April 1939)

That grand old man, Edwin Caldwell, now in his ninety-fourth year, became Postmaster of Hopton Wafers in 1893 when the office first opened. He has a remarkable memory. Not long ago he told me of the days when Hopton Wafers and other hamlets on the slopes of Clee Hill were without a postman of any kind until at last an old countryman made it his pleasure (for profit) to walk to Cleobury Mortimer and gather from the Post Office there any letters for people living in the Hopton Wafers and Clee Hill country.

"Of course," Edwin Caldwell stroked his beard and chuckled as he spoke, "of course, he'd never bring the letters for folk who didn't pay a few coppers, just what they thought right; there was no fixed charge. So, you see, our first postman took the job on himself — made his own rules, too. Country lads are not so green as some of them look — oh, no!"

"What I'd like to see again," went on the old man, "what I often think about are the old coaches. Down the hill yonder they came, the horses in a rare sweat, to the Crown yard" — he pointed across a small triangular green field to the old inn snuggled in a hollow near the brook. "The horn would sound — a grand tone the coaching horn had — and out would come the ostler with fresh horses all ready — change over — and off they'd go across the Clee to Ludlow; that road climbs to over 1,200 feet above sea-level. The arrival and departure of that coach would stir your blood more than all the mail vans on the road to-day."

While talking to the old man I began to wonder how many miles some of the rural postmen of long ago walked in a day's march. I feel sure that in the old days letters were "letters"; I mean, football coupons, sale notices, shopping by post and all the host of O.H.M.S. correspondence had not arrived. All letters were, I suppose, first-class correspondence so that, although the postman's load might not be a big one, the distance he walked would surprise the bus-riding, motoring people of to-day.

A Clee Hill farmer's wife I know has, from time to time, told many tales of one stalwart of the days gone by. Edwin Broome was not his name but it will serve; he was a man who kept his kindness and thoughtfulness hidden beneath a gruff unceremonious manner; he would have the people know that he was His Majesty's official Letter Carrier, a man of importance in this quiet countryside. A tall, fine figure of a man he was, always spotlessly clean and well booted, and he always wore an old-fashioned starched "butterfly" collar, his big Adam's apple protruding through the "wings." In bad weather he carried a big umbrella of which he was very proud.

It seemed, so my informer said, as if Edwin Broome believed he had a perfect right to read all postcards, and when he delivered a letter he would, more often than not, question and cross-examine the recipient until all the news it contained, or the letter itself, was passed on to him — His Majesty's official Letter Carrier.

It happened that a farmer's daughter, a very charming girl, had become engaged to a young man who lived in a distant town. His work was connected with printing and engraving. It soon became known to this young couple that Edwin Broome read, very carefully, every postcard which passed between them. The young man, more amused than annoyed, supplied his fiancée with a magnifying glass and told her to wait and see. The writing on the next card addressed to the girl was very small, so small, indeed, that it was impossible to read it without the aid of a good magnifying glass. But all the writing was not so minute. At the bottom of the carl old Edwin Broome, His Majesty's official Letter Carrier, saw, in big bold handwriting, these words -

> *"I will tell you the other news when I see you.*
> *I am sure old Edwin Broome reads all he can   Love, Tom".*

It was Edwin's custom to walk into the kitchen of the farmhouse where the girl lived. On the day when this card arrived his step was heavier and quicker than usual; he swung the kitchen door open and stamped into the flagged room with a look of mingled scorn and indignation on his face. His eyes flashed, his blood was up. He glared at the family — they were seated at breakfast — and then he flung the offending card on to the table.

"It's a lie!" he shouted as he thumped the corner of the heavy oak table. "It's a lie — a damned lie!"

Then he turned and stamped his way out of the house, leaving all who were seated there — except one girl who controlled her laughter with a great effort — wondering at the cause of his outburst, and asking each other why he had gone without drinking the very excellent cup of tea which was always poured out for him as he approached the house.

An incident of this kind helps to support my belief that the postmen of yesterday and today are not so careless and indifferent about the contents of the letters they carry as they were supposed to be in Cowper's day. In the opening stanza of Book IV of *The Task*, Cowper wrote -

> "He comes, the herald of a noisy world,
> With spattered boots, strapp'd waist, frozen locks,
> News from all nations lumbering at his back.
> True to his charge the close pack'd load behind,
> Yet careless what he brings, his one concern
> Is to conduct it to the destined inn,
> And having dropp'd the expected bag — pass on
> He whistles as he goes, light-hearted wretch,
> Cold and yet cheerful: messenger of grief
> Perhaps to thousands, and of joy to some,
> To him indifferent whether grief or joy."

No, I for one do not believe it. In country places it might almost be said that the length of hill and dale which makes up the postman's walk is, for him, his little world and, even if his powers of observation are weak, he must know that in many instances good news is expected and people are always eager and anxious to read what will confirm their hopes. I sometimes thank that people "sense" bad news; the letter is accepted with some hesitation, turned over and over and examined as if some mistake has been made. Still, in spite of bills, income tax demand notes and other uninteresting matter, the postman is always welcome — the world, it seems to me, is living in hope. Almost everyone is expecting a letter, but so few people know where they expect their letters to come from I'm really not surprised that so many are disappointed.

These disappointments, however, do not stop them from expecting good news from somewhere. "Hope springs eternal in the human breast." If old Edwin Broome were alive to-day I wonder what his thoughts would be if he could peep into, say, Liverpool or Manchester Head Office when tens of thousands of circulars and a "rush" of football coupons were being handled.

I think the postman is more familiar to-day than any other uniformed official. How is it that he has not been given a nickname? In his essay *Double Knock*, E.V. Lucas makes a suggestion.

"The soldier," he wrote, "is Tommy, the sailor is Jack, the policeman is Robert; but we have no familiar word for the postman, although he is nearer our hearts than any of those others. What could he be called? Nothing seems to fit, but I should not vote against Andy. In fact, I think Andy rather good."

LETTERS
(from *The Post Office Magazine* July 1939)

When we read that the Post Office deals with so many millions of letters — indeed, even when we see tens of thousands of letters stacked on desks, few of us, I imagine, are really interested. I am not suggesting that Post Office people do not give any thought to their work; what I mean is, almost all men are more interested in their own personal mail than they are in, say, 50,000 letters going north, south, east and west.

For instance, a postcard I had this morning from Quetta gave me a good deal more pleasure than the thousands of letters I sorted while on duty last week. During our daily walks in town or country we meet thousands of men and women, but it is only now and then that we come across a rare character — a really great man, or a really comic fellow. And so it is with letters. Most of us have received more letters than we care to remember, but only now and then have we had the pleasure of opening a very unexpected letter — a letter we count as a great honour, or a letter which gives us good cause for loud and hearty laughter.

I have some six letters from a man who is a great lover of the English countryside: he was our Prime Minister. I am very proud of his letters; they encouraged me to persevere in work I had set myself to do. Some years ago I received a long letter — 44 pages of closely-written, neat handwriting: this is easily the most interesting and instructive letter I have ever had. The writer, an elderly scholar unknown to me, begged me to call on him but — as Belloc would say — although I still have his letter, I have never spoken to him, for I never saw him, nor shall I see him, nor he me, until the Great Day.

The most humorous letter I ever read was not my own — I saw it by chance. A young officer of my Regiment called me across to where he sat —we were a few miles behind Ypres. He was censoring letters written by men of my company.

"Look at that," he said, and he threw a letter towards me. "Now what ought I to do with that? Let it go — or — ?"

The letter was from an elderly, rough diamond of a fellow — the Old Crow, we called him — to his wife. What that man wrote was perfectly true — I have never forgotten his letter — but I must not repeat a word of it. It certainly was the best war-time letter I ever saw or heard about. If things are running crossways, if the world looks grey, I think of this letter; it never fails to make me chuckle. I hope the Old Crow is as happy as he deserves to be.

Another good war-time letter is the following cheerful effort from a young member of the B.E.F.:-

"Dear Mum and Dad, and loving sisters Rose,
Mabel and our Gladys, I am very pleased to write
you another welcome letter as this leaves me at
present. Dear Mum and Dad and loving sisters,
keep the home-fires burning. Not arf! The boys
are in the pink. Not arf! Dear loving sisters, Rose,
Mabel and our Gladys, keep merry and bright. Not
arf!"

That, I think is the real thing; it comes straight from the heart. Is the lad who
wrote it as cheerful now as he was then? I wonder.

And now back from the war to Shropshire. Some time ago the squire's wife
gave me a copy of a letter she had from two brothers, elderly farm-hands and
faithful servants to the old squire for many years. The mother of the two men
and the squire died on the same day. This fact drew from the men the following
note:-

"From T. P. & B. P. to Mises Tudor

dear Mises Tudor.

i rites to tel you as pore muther wat was yure frend bin gon ded an me an hour ben
is al alon an we ave not got nuthink. We bin very sory tere as mister Tudor bin gon
ded. Opes e gon teven.

yure truely,

Ted & ben plunket."

The handwriting of the original is remarkable and uncommon; it was, I am
sure, a literary effort that cost a good deal of thought. I sometimes wish I had
a collection of such letters; they help us to see the times in which they were
written, and they help us to see the men and women who lived in those times.

For many years I exchanged letters with a man who roamed all over the face
of the world. He was a good letter-writer. His letters were, for me, more
interesting than any travel book I have ever read. It seems to me that few men
realise what a wonderful service they have at a very small cost. The collection,
sorting, dispatch and delivery of letters are accepted as part of everyday life. Soon
after we come into the world we realise that there is a postal service and, although
we make use of it, we give it very little thought. Dr. Johnson, however, found
time to observe and make some comment on almost everything. Boswell said
(of Dr. Johnson), "As he opened a note which his servant brought him, he said,
'An odd thought strikes me: we shall receive no letters in the grave.'"

A letter of complaint of the railway company probably brought a smile to the
face of the most unhappy director. A man bought a house close to a railway
station; soon afterwards he wrote to the company -

"Gentlemen,

Why must your engines ding & dong & bang & fizz & spit & pant & grate & grind & puff & bump & chug & hoot & toot & whistle & wheeze & jar & jerk & snarl & slam & throb & roar & rattle & yell & smell & smoke & shriek & SCREAM all the night long?

Yours, etc."

A letter which gave me many happy moments came from a native on the North-West Frontier of India: his name I have never been able to decipher. This letter was addressed to:-

The Honourable Simon Evans,

Postman of Shropshire,

England.

The scrawled handwriting, the large ornate capitals, the thin foreign note-paper and several stamps sprawled on the back of the envelope — all these caught my eye first of all. And, I thought to myself, if the Honourable Evans really was the Postman of Shropshire, he would be a very busy man. However, I am better known than I thought I was, for the letter arrived without delay at Cleobury Mortimer.

The writer of this letter, whose name is still a mystery, wanted to know if I would be kind and honourable, and, he said, he knew that in my goodness I would send him a few samples of my books. I was assured that any books by the Honourable Simon Evans would be welcomed with a smile. All this was a pleasant surprise, but there was a still greater surprise in store. The postscript was the gem of the whole letter:-

"Postscript, after-thought" (he wrote), "And, Dear Sir, will you also be kind and honourable and send, with the books you post register to me, a note to let me know how much for Mr. Shakespeare and who is the author."

Now and then it is possible to make a good guess at the contents of a letter. How they are received gives us a clue. I remember a charming young lady who when the postman arrived at her home early in the morning, would dash down the wide staircase holding up her pyjamas — or, to use her own expression, girding up her loins — and shouting for joy. If the all important letter was among the morning mail she would give a loud whoop and disappear up the stairs, still girding her loins. These letters came at regular intervals and, regarding their contents, I know my guess was a good one because — she told me so.

What makes a good letter? It is difficult to say. I remember reading somewhere or other: "The style of letters ought to be free, easy and natural; as near approaching familiar conversation as possible. The two best qualities in conversation are good humour and good breeding. Those letters are therefore certainly the best that show the most of these two qualities." That, it seems to me, sums the matter up very well.

AN OLD COUNTRYMAN TO HIS SON
(from *Country Life* 1 July 1939)

I've be'n thinkin' a good deal o' this thing an' that,
Now, listen awhile, I'ull tell thee what's what.
These be turrible times lad — I'ud have thee draw nigh,
An' I'ull tell thee a wrinkle or two by an' by.

They'm goin' too fast lad, I tell thee, a deal,
Our tuth-three new neighbours — they'm agrowin' o' keel,*
An' what dost thee think they'ull be doin' jus' now?
Why, they'ull up an' they'ull laugh at the old wooden plough!

These new-fangled farmers, them as drinks at the Lion,
They say as they wants 'um, an' all things, o 'iron!
"Iron!" they shouts, "iron we'ull have!" An' wood there's no trade for.
Surree! What do folks think as ash trees be made for?

There be some as'ull put two girt hosses abreast,
An' they'ull holler "Gee-ho!" an' "Gee-hup!" an' the rest;
I warrants they'ull call 'um for long an' enow,
But I tell thee Tom lad, that way'ull ne'er do.

Now gi'e I a good wooden plough as is strong,
An' a pair o' good wheels to help her along,
An' three long tailed tits,** a man an' a lad,
A good steady pace an' it shanna be bad.

Now, Thomas my lad, dunna heed what they say
But get thee along in thy faither's old way;
Their manner o' workin' spells ruin, I trow,
So stick, while you live, to the old wooden plough,
   The old wooden plough to be sure.

*Keel, *kale.* ** Tits, *horses.*

HELD UP!
(from *The Post Office Magazine* August 1939)

Morris Minor van 0527 had done almost 50,000 miles and still went fairly well. I was nearing home after my journey up the Valley of the Rea and over the high roads that cross the open common land on the eastern slopes of Clee Hill. I'd called at five small sub-offices and cleared a number of roadside letter boxes. As I approached Crump's Brook box I knew I was just about on time — perhaps a minute or two early. Crump's Brook runs down from somewhere near Cleeton St. Mary on the higher slopes of Clee. The letter box, clamped to a stout post almost in the heather that grows down to the very edge of the road, had been in position only one day; it had been put there for the use of the few cottagers who live round about.

I stopped the van, opened the door, and prepared to unfold myself from about the steering wheel, when a tall man I'd never seen before jumped from behind a clump of gorse and hurried through the heather towards me. He had an inquisitive, happy face and he wore a smile not unlike Mr. Pickwick's. He was fairly well dressed, his bowler hat was on his head at a rather jaunty angle, his bright red neck-tie was of the latest style. I noticed that the pockets of his big overcoat were full and heavy and, although the breeze kept the coat wide open, I felt quite sure that with his right hand he was holding on to something in his overcoat pocket.

I always feel helpless when I'm at the wheel of a small car; on this occasion I felt even more helpless than usual. If ever you see a man who turns the scale at about 15 stone and stands 6 feet 2 in his socks, and that man is seated at the wheel of a Morris Minor van, you will agree, I think, that about the only thing he *can* do is — drive. He can't fight — not in that position, at any rate.

And so I sat — with my knees up, my elbows out, and the wheel against my chest — looking at this big man who smiled at me in a way — on second thoughts — that I did not like; it was such a superior, self-satisfied smile, and yet the man seemed friendly enough. He looked like one of the hail-fellow-well-met kind who would find a real delight in cracking a bottle with a friend. But why did he keep that right hand of his hidden so deep in his overcoat pocket?

On the films, and in real life, I believe there are men who shoot from the pocket. And gangsters in the flesh are, perhaps, ordinary looking men, not unlike this fellow who stood only a yard or so away watching me intently with that fixed smile still on his face.

"Well," he said at last, and now he stood so near I could not put my foot out of the van without treading on his toes, "well, and what time do you clear this box?" he asked.

As the box had only just been put in position I did not know what time was showing on the plate. I did know, however, that I always passed this spot at about

4.15 p.m. — so I said that the box was cleared at 4.10 or 4.15 p.m. but I was not sure of this. I added that the time of clearance ought to be shown on the time-plate, and that this box was a new one.

"Aha!" — the fellow did not move, his right hand seemed to go deeper into his pocket and whatever he held there moved — "aha!" he chuckled, "you ought to be able to answer my question without looking at the box — surely you know what time you collect here?"

"Well," I replied — then, suddenly, I forced myself out of the van and took a peep at the box, "yes — I ought to know — and I do know. I clear this box at 4.15 — never before 4.15 p.m."

"Aha!" he laughed again and moved a few inches, "Oho — but you had to take a look at the box before you could answer. Now, tell me, was Dick Turpin hung at York or Tyburn?"

"Dick Turpin — Dick Turpin" I said, trying to size the fellow up, "well — I don't know. The truth is, I'm not very interested — I don't think it matters very much."

"Aha, you're not interested — eh?" — his smile became almost sinister — "you know, of course, that Dick Turpin was a highwayman?" As he said this he stepped close to me.

"Oh, yes, that's true enough," I said as I moved quickly towards the box.

Then the fellow stepped in my way. I saw his right hand move but he still kept it in his pocket; he sidled round and stood close by my side. His overcoat pocket touched me and I felt something hard pressing against my hip.

"Now," he said quietly, "I'll tell you something — something you can bet on. Dick Turpin was hung at York — not Tyburn."

"Well," I said roughly, "I don't care a tinker's cuss who claims Dick Turpin as their hero." The fellow backed a little and looked surprised, then he smiled again. "Anyhow," I went on, "why bring up this question about Dick Turpin? What's he got to do with you — or me?"

"My friend," the reply came with a chuckle, "my friend, you don't like Dick — our famous Dick Turpin, do you?"

"No," I said, and to tell the truth, nor did I like the way that hidden right hand moved. I became certain that whatever it was he held so grimly was pointing at me.

"Well," he laughed aloud, "well — what about Oliver Cromwell? He was — "

"What's your big idea?" I asked, "I've no time to answer questions. As to Cromwell — if you listen to some folk — he's been almost everywhere doing all sorts of things. What about Elizabeth, Queen Elizabeth, there's thousands of good old beds up and down the country — if you believe what you hear — Elizabeth slept in every one of them. That kind of talk might add to the value of the beds — but I doubt if Elizabeth slept in a different bed every night of her life."

As I finished this long speech I turned and cleared the box. When I turned towards the van again the man stood facing me, his smile was as friendly as ever but he was struggling to withdraw his hand from his overcoat pocket. Now — I wondered — what next?

"Listen!" — the man grabbed my arm with his left hand; he spoke quietly now. I shook myself free and prepared to defend myself — "listen," he went on, "listen to me — who said this?

> "Life is real! Life is earnest!
> And the grave is not its goal.
> 'Dust thou art, to dust returnest,'
> Was not written of the soul."

"Longfellow," I said, "Longfellow — the American."

"Wrong!" he shouted.

"No — I'm right," I said.

"Wrong!" he shouted louder than before, "here, my friend," he succeeded at last in withdrawing his hand from his pocket, and then I saw what he held.

It was a bottle! A bottle full of good old tawny port. All the time it had been the neck of that bottle he'd been pointing at me.

"Now," he yelled, and produced, as if by magic, a corkscrew, "now, my friend, draw the cork I say, draw the cork and let us drink."

For a moment I was too surprised to move, then I chuckled, jumped into the little van and drove away. I left that queer fellow standing near a bank of heather, a bottle of port in one hand, a corkscrew in the other, and a smile on his face.

COUNTRYMEN
(from *Country Life* 4 January 1941)

It is in the local inn that one hears all about gardening. Old Tom Tallents seldom speaks, but when he does he almost always says something interesting and to the point.

"Aha," he said last Saturday night, "if my 'taters be as good as they wur las' year I 'ull be content — white as a hound's tooth they wur."

With those few words — white as a hound's tooth — old Tom described good sound potatoes better than any seed catalogue or gardening book that has ever come my way; indeed, I do not think a great scholar could find a phrase so expressive, so unmistakable in its meaning. Many countrymen have this gift. They speak in a simple, direct way, and they hit the nail on the head. It is, I suppose, this natural directness, this straight-forward thinking, that helps to make what are known as "country characters."

It seems to me that there are more characters in the country than there are in town. The reason for this is that townsmen are more conventional. To look odd or eccentric seems to weigh against a man in town, and the fact that townsmen are almost always on the move, always in a hurry, anxious to do something or ready to be amused, robs them of a trait that is still strong in the make-up of the countryman. Nothing pleases a countryman more than to be left alone, to be allowed to do his work in his own way.

In spite of modern machinery the seasons — spring, summer, autumn and winter — come as ever they did; we can neither hurry nor delay them. Prophets may prophesy and scientists may expound, but the weather remains as uncertain as the wind, and what a countryman turns his hand to depends on the season, the wind and the weather. If he can, a true countryman will stay in or near the village or among the hills where he was cradled, and so he has time to grow and develop in a natural way; he keeps his rough edges and colour; he is not "regimented," nor has he got what might be called the "factory mind." I am not suggesting that countrymen are clever — no, the clever men come from the towns and universities — but it seems to me that there are more wise men in the country than there are anywhere else. For ready wit and good humour give me the countryman every time.

Some years ago I found a good deal of pleasure on my holidays by going from one little market town to another. In any stretch of country you will find that market days do not clash. (For instance, in the country hereabouts, there is a market at Ludlow on Mondays, at Tenbury on Tuesdays, at Cleobury Mortimer on Wednesdays, at Kidderminster on Thursdays and so on.) At cattle sales and markets countrymen gather together; they make their market days a kind of entertainment, fairly put themselves to it and sharpen their wits on the wits of their neighbours.

Country characters, the brightest of them, are very interesting fellows. They are the salt of the countryside. I fancy that townsmen seldom see countrymen at their best. (I am fortunate in having opportunities of mixing with countrymen as one of themselves.) If a man calls at an inn right in the heart of the country he may do his best to put the company at ease, and they may appear to be perfectly natural, but he is a stranger among them and they are aware of his presence. I have, many times, been one of the company in an inn when a stranger — a well dressed or fairly well dressed townsman — has walked in. After some talk he may think he is one of the company; the chaff and banter may be as loud as it was an hour before, but I know these countrymen well enough to be sure that, in spite of appearances, they are rather like children pretending to be at ease. They are not perfectly natural. A stranger is always a stranger, and a countryman is almost always on guard. Why anyone attempts to write a novel of the country unless he or she has lived in the country for many years puzzles me. Long ago someone said: "If you wish to write a great novel of Shropshire, go to Shropshire and live among the Shropshire people." This is good advice, and it is, of course, true of any other part of England.

How long must a man live among country people before he begins to know them well, before he is accepted as one of themselves? This is not an easy question to answer. People who are able to spend long holidays in the country might like to think about this. I have no doubt that a good deal depends on the man himself — he must be patient and good-humoured, broad-minded and tolerant. Country characters are born, not made; if you are accepted by them you are indeed fortunate.

Some townsmen make the mistake of thinking that a country character is a sort of show-piece, a kind of comedian provided to entertain strangers. This is all wrong. You must treat country people as you find them, as fellow-men. Sometimes when in the taproom of my favourite inn I feel that old Omar Khayyam knew all about it. In my mind's eye I see the Potter's Shop and the Clay Population:

> And strange to tell, among that Earthern Lot
> Some could articulate, while others not:
>   And suddenly one more impatient cried -
> "Who is the Potter, pray, and who the Pot?"
>
> None answered this; but after Silence spake
> A Vessel of a more ungainly Make:
>   "They sneer at me for leaning all awry;
> What! did the Hand then of the Potter shake?"

And there, it seems to me, is the thought that lies in the heart of the countryman; he wants to be accepted without question. Whether he is bent or upright, full of wit or dry as a stick, he is natural growth and he wants to be himself. His way of living, his thinking, his speech, his dress — all are part of

45

10, 11: With Edward Onslow — photographs taken by Norman Thompson Williams in 1934. (Marilyn Howells)

the man himself. A search for characters is seldom, if ever, successful. All the odd incidents I have seen and all the queer old men I count as my friends have come my way by accident, by chance.

An old countryman, knotted as an oak and with a face as set as if hewn out of mahogany, is not always as solid and humourless as he looks. I remember in the kitchen of an inn, seeing a shy-looking old ploughman play a trick on a visitor from town. The stranger had been asking questions and, as he thought, fooling the countrymen. After putting up with the fellow for some time the old ploughman said, quietly and with some hesitation, that he had a trick, and he agreed, in a half-hearted way, to let the smart stranger have a go at it. He called for a quart of cider — the stranger paid. Then the old man climbed on to a chair and placed the brim-full quart pot against the ceiling; he asked the stranger to pick up a short stick and hold the quart pot tight against the ceiling. With his arm at full length the man could just manage this. Then the ploughman said: "Now, surree, the trick is: yow mun get away an' kep dry," and without a trace of a smile he went out. The landlord disappeared, the company sat back and watched. A few minutes later a rather damp and bad-tempered man climbed into his car and went away.

One of the most interesting characters I have ever met was a man named William Pratt. He was, for a few months, the landlord of the local inn. At the inn a club met once a week. Almost every village has one these clubs. There is a good deal of ceremony attached to them, a special way of knocking for admission, pass-words, and so on. Old William Pratt hated secrecy; he wanted everything plain, straight and open. He made no attempt to close the club, but his remarks about it were, to put it mildly, rather rude. One night when the club met William went off down a lane behind the inn to a field where a donkey, a she-ass, had a little foal. William was a big, strong man; he picked up the baby ass and carried it back to the inn. He astonished his customers by going to the door of the room where the meeting was being held. He gave the secret knock. The door opened, and someone shouted: "Give the pass-word!" Old William stepped boldly into the room, hoisted the little ass on to the table and pushed it forward. "Brother Ass!" he shouted, "a new member — without the pass-word!"

SECTION THREE

This section contains two articles by Evans which have never been published before. They are taken from his one surviving notebook. Doubtless Evans would have refined and improved these before publication. For present purposes, a certain amount of editing has been necessary, but this has been kept to a minimum.

'DOCTOR' PALMER

Not long ago, I walked from Cleobury Mortimer by way of Nineveh, Shakenhurst Woods and Mamble to Frith Common to see old George Palmer. George Palmer is known for miles around as 'Doctor Palmer' — I asked him why. He told me that he had been called 'Doctor' ever since he sang a song about a real Dr Palmer many many years ago. George Palmer's 99th birthday is not far away, but apart from a rheumaticky stiff leg, he's as spry and lively as a man of 60 or so, and he's always happy and cheerful.

Now what strikes me every time I meet old Mr Palmer is this: it's almost impossible to surprise a really old man. Last time I called on him he was pottering about his garden and I said I ought to have let him know that I was calling.

"Eh, no lad, no," he said. "You come when you'd a mind to come, you'm allus welcome." Then — he's a very short man and I'm rather tall — he cocked his head on one side like a wise old bird and looked up at me with a merry twinkle in his eye and went on — "Come whenever you'd a mind, lad, 'cos here we'm allus the same — yesterday, to-day an' tomorrow we'm the same."

He's a good talker is old Doctor, wise and witty, and it's good to meet a very old man who is really happy and interested in life. I don't think I've ever met a man more interested in his garden. Some old men live in the past but here is a man who, although he loves to talk about the past, will have his joke about the things of to-day — about aeroplanes and fashions and modern dancing and crooners.

His memories of life eighty and ninety years ago are fresh and vivid. He left school at nine years of age and went to work on a farm. It's strange to think that I've had lots of talk with a man who left school in the year 1850.

Every time there's a pause in the conversation, Dr Palmer begins to beat with his hand and then, in a voice as clear as a bell, he sings little snatches of song, and always when he sings his face keeps lighting up with smiles and his eyes seem to dance with joy.

He told me of his work when he was a lad scaring birds off the wheat, and of the dances all about the countryside. He never missed one, although he had to walk miles. "I worked hard," he said "but many's the wet shirt I've had — *dancing*, an' I were allus fond o' singing — would you like to hear an old song?" he asked. Of course I would and so I had one: 'Jemima'.

To talk with someone who has *seen* the past and *lived* in it is better than reading about it. Old Dr Palmer told me of the stage waggon that brought supplies from Worcester and London. He told me of the stage coach, its four horses and the lively sound of the horn as it came up the valley of the Teme just below his cottage. And a wonderful story he told me of how a stage coach driver managed to escape from the flooded river — the highest flood they'd ever had there — by driving hard, "like a madman," he said. When he tells a story his hands and arms move and his eyes light up with the memory of it all.

He married when he was a young man earning one shilling and sixpence a day but, he said, he went for the biggest pay and became a builder's labourer and hod carrier at fourpence an hour. This work took him to the town where he found good lodgings at three shillings a week. After a few years at that he came back to the country again and worked on a big farm for two shillings a day, and in addition he had two quarts of small beer allowed him. What a queer sight it would be if we saw the country as it was in his day, rutted roads and slow moving traffic, all the farm hands in wonderful smocks and gangs of Irishmen and Welshmen moving about the country at harvest time. These were the mowing gangs and good men they were too. The Irishmen, Dr Palmer told me, used sickles and the Welshmen broad hooks, and although they were up at work before the dawn the Welshmen would sing almost all night.

We were having a cup of tea by now; tea and toast is now the old man's favourite meal. "I like tea," he said, "many a time I went to the shop when I was a lad for half an ounce of tea, a penny ha'penny it was for half an ounce."

We talked about the food they had in the old days and I said that perhaps in this wooded country they made all their fires of wood. But no — I was wrong — some small pits not far way, he said, sold coal for seven shillings a ton, or sixpence for a big wheel barrow load, or a penny for as much as a man could carry on his back. Coal gave the old man his opportunity — the old man can sing about almost anything. "I know a song about coal," he said, "'Down among the Coal' it's called."

Breakfast for farm hands in those old days was a basin of bacon broth and a cup of cider. At one place, the old man told me with a chuckle, they had a little cheese now and then, but it was so hard that when the farmer's wife was not looking the men took it out to the block and knocked a few pieces off with the hacker.

Dancing must have given Dr Palmer great pleasure. Modern dancing, he says, is not dancing at all. "The best dancer I ever met," he said, "was a girl on Clee Hill — she *could* dance — many an hour we danced together, Roger de Coverley and Drops o' Brandy — she were a smart 'un."

I asked him how the girls dressed at these dances. "Oho," he said, "they were like they be now — fond o' being in fashion but they wore crinolines then and they must ha' been heavy — yards and yards o' flounces all around 'em an' lots of whale bone. Hats, too," he said, "were allus charming in those days — just as they be now. I used to sing about one o' the hat fashions, he went on, and at once he began to beat time to 'Flippy Floppy Hat'.

He told me of the annual Hiring Fair at Cleobury on the 2nd of May. Shepherds would wear some sheep's wool in their button hole, and waggoners would carry or wear a whip. When a man was hired for the year he was given a shilling; this shilling sealed the deal — he was engaged. Some farmers would tie a ribbon in the coat of the man they'd hired.

When he was a young man, he was happy at one place; he had a good bed, good food and the girl would bring him a jug of cider as often as he wanted it. From this place he had many journeys to town with loads of cider —four hogsheads — or loads of wheat. They had to pay a toll to cross the Severn at Bewdley, and as they saved a little money by returning the same day, they often set out from the Teme valley about midnight or soon after. "Yes," he agreed, he had had a hard life but he'd enjoyed it. Singing must have helped to keep him happy. When he was a boy scaring birds he sang 'The Barley Mow' — the first song his father taught him — and he sings it now with as much pleasure as he sang it ninety years ago.

He told me of times when, after a wet season when the wheat sprouted, and the bread was so bad that when it was thrown against the wall, it would stick there. But, after telling me of something bad he always thought of something good. "Life," he said, "is a mixture of good and bad," and he believed in finding as much of the good as possible and making the best of it. With his wife and children he'd been happy. He'd always kept a couple of good pigs and when they were fat, and ready for killing, one was sold and the other was killed and cured. Too much red tape and law-making these days he said — every man ought to have his own roof over his head, and his own garden. Then he sang a song that he said was a bit of good advice for the girls.

UNCLE NED

On my postman's walk I meet some old countrymen of great quality. I enclose a sketch of one grand old man. His attitude towards life and his thoughts may help men and women who do not possess his strength of character, his loyalty, and his devotion to his master — the land.

*   *   *   *

I find it difficult to believe that some of the weather-beaten solid old men I meet on and about the Clee Hills were ever little children. They look as if they have always been old, always been as they are now, and always will be. Many of them are men of great quality; they have a natural dignity and the perfect manners that always seem to go with it. Strong personalities they are, with strong kindly faces and a keen sense of humour. They may not be clever but they are wise, they live near the heart of things, and they belong to the field and fold, to the forge and homely workshop. They have cultivated the wise habits of their forefathers, and know that the enduring things of life cannot be hurried in the making.

It is my duty to walk up the valley and over the hills every day in all kinds of wind and weather. I meet and talk with — 'these men of pith and thew whom the city never called'.

Outstanding among these old men is Edward Hembury. For many years I have called him Uncle Ned although at the back of my mind I always think of him as Corduroy Ned. I have never met him anywhere but in the fields or in his cottage. He always wears corduroy clothes — coat, waistcoat, trousers and billycock hat. He keeps himself and his clothes as neat and clean as a good soldier. At 81 years of age he is upright and strong. Something about him, perhaps his snow white hair and his strong corduroy clothes always makes me think of healthy winter weather but in spite of his rugged tough unsmiling appearance he is a kindly gentle old man. He lives alone, his cottage is always spotlessly clean and he loves a big bright fire. "Ay suree," I have often heard him say, "It's bin a gran' summer but I'm glad it's past and gone. I likes a good fire wi' a blaze — it's kind o' friendly when I sit here o' nights by mysel'".

I called on him one evening not long ago. He opened his cottage door before I reached it, stepped forward, shook my hand and motioned me in. When I made myself comfortable in one his ladder-back chairs, he poured out two glasses of dandelion wine. We smoked and talked for a while then he said "You bin sure, I lives easy now an' I thinks a lot."

These few words set *me* thinking because I know the old man does a good deal of hedging and ditching, a little rabbiting, and some shepherding as well as other odd jobs for farmers who live round about, and he spends a good deal of his time gathering brushwood and cordwood for his fire — all this in addition to looking after his cottage and half an acre or so of garden. Yet I have his word for it that he lives easy and thinks a lot!

"Ah," he said after a pause, "Ah — I'm glad you'm called." "Why?" I asked, "Another tale to tell me?" "No," Uncle Ned straightened his back and stared into the fire, "No — not 'zackly a tale — I bin thinking." "Good for you," I said, "Go ahead, Uncle Ned, you've something on your mind."

Uncle Ned sipped his wine and went on. "An' o' this I be sartin sure — the land's a hard master but a good one. Ay — the land's the real gaffer. Look about an' see how folks treat it — acres o' dock, an' briar, an' thistle. Why? Why? I'll tell you — folks is troubled about money an' easy ways o' makin' it. Maybe it's money as makes the mare to go — but it's corn as makes her gallop. I say as there's too many big hedges about — too much living — corn we wants, more corn. Ower an' ower agen I heard my old father say "Buy grain and sow," he'd say, "the good old earth 'ull pay you back a hundred fold." I hear folks say as Guvment gives too many orders. But I say as there inna too many orders — no — but for many a year ther've bin the wrong orders. I say as all the country ought to be as clean as a cottage garden — made the best use on — not let go wild an' thistle-dy in great patches. An' I say as men dunna leave the fields to go an' work wi' gangs o' men in a great shed place full o' noise and dust wi'out good reason. A man as knows his horses — a man as knows the order o' the work as comes in a twelve month — a man as knows the ways o' sheep and' cattle, an' all the jobs as must be done right and proper — he dunna go an' live in a house like a box agen big chimneys and trams and things — not wi'out good reason. Give a man wages as 'ull stop him from worriting — an' give him work as he can take a pride in — then he 'ull be happy an' thank God for his work. All manner o' things come an' go, but the land goes on, surree, it never changes, no, it never changes if men 'ud do as they ought to do — work. An' men ought to be proud to stand agin their job an' say — "this is the work I ha' done.""

* * * * *

Editor's note: This article has much in common with 'Corduroy Ned', which may be found on pages 40-45 of *Shropshire Days and Shropshire Ways*. However, it is well worth including here as in this version Uncle Ned's thoughts are significantly more far-reaching than in the later version included in *Shropshire Days*.

SECTION FOUR

This final section is devoted to articles written about Simon Evans during his lifetime or soon after his death. Although the first item, 'Walking Post Offices', refers to a postman called 'Mr. Burns', circumstantial evidence suggests that the author is in fact writing about Simon Evans.

WALKING POST OFFICES
by 'Quaestor' (Wilfred Byford-Jones)
(from his book *Midland Leaves*, published in 1934)

The postman blows a whistle and waits. The shrill notes go rocketing through the lonely valley. A herd of white-faced Hereford cattle cease grazing and look up as though annoyed that the song of the birds and the ripple of the River Rea should be spoiled by so vulgar a noise.

Why the postman should blow a whistle at this spot may seem a mystery to some people, for the narrow, hedged lanes appear to lead to nowhere but that primeval volcano, Titterstone Clee Hill, on the one side, and through meadows that stretch into limitless distance on the other. But cottages and stock farms are hidden away in sequestered vales in this uneven country. The postman must whistle and wait — wait in case anyone wishes to give him letters, buy stamps, or dog, wireless, or gun licences, or postal or money orders.

The postmen who travel through the Clee Hills district are walking post offices. Owing to the fact that the countryside is so sparingly populated, and that houses are so widely scattered, not even post boxes can be provided at convenient distances, not to mention post offices. One delivery and a collection of letters and parcels occupy a man from seven o'clock in the morning to five o'clock at night. Some of the rounds are the loneliest and most interesting in all England.

The postman waits. The cows have continued to graze. The river ripples on beneath the overhanging bushes of pink and white may, which, together with the blazing sunshine, cast fascinating reflections on the water's surface. Birds of many and rare varieties sing in the trees and hedgerows and high up in the clear blue sky.

Presently there is a shout.

A labourer in the fields far away waves a hoe.

There are letters.

In a few moments a little girl comes running down the lane.

"Hallo, Mary," the postman greets her.

He knows the names of everyone on his round.

"Hallo, Mr. Burns."

Instead of putting three pennies and three half-pennies in a slot and posting the stamped letters in a pillar-box as we would do in town, the girl buys the stamps from the postman and hands him the letters. He slings his bag over his shoulder and sets off again down the lane.

•　•　•　•　•

The Clee Hills district is peopled by an agricultural stock which seems to be a civilisation apart. The labourers, farmers and cattle raisers and their womenfolk live lonely lives. Some of them may go for days without seeing the face of a stranger. Long ago Saxon and Celt fused to produce these hardy, reticent, lovable people, and they have remained here through the centuries. One feels that they are the real English, their country the real England.

You will not find them by walking through the lanes — nothing short of taking their letters will give you a glimpse of them, of their old stone cottages, some with rye thatches and scalloped eaves, of farms built of local material, stone quarried in the Clee Hills and wood hewn down in the forests, of their quaint furniture, clothes, habits. They are all reminders of an age unhurried by invention.

12: The mischievous smile – an early publicity photograph. (Doris Aldridge-Evans)

At about six o'clock in the morning a van arrives at Cleobury Mortimer Post Office. It has been driven from Kidderminster, twelve miles away, and contains the letters and parcels for the people scattered over an area of about one hundred square miles. The nearest towns, other than Kidderminster, are Bridgnorth, fourteen miles away, and Ludlow, eleven miles away. The letters are at once sorted into "walks" in the post office next to a grocer's shop, which is kept by the postmaster. At about seven o'clock they are taken out by full-time and part-time postmen.

The full-time men go on long journeys of between fifteen and seventeen miles. The part-time men, among them a chimney sweep, ostler, huckster, rabbit catcher and potman, do shorter rounds, and they return to their chimneys, horses, rabbits and shops.

Overnight in a local inn I asked a full-time postman if I could accompany him on his walk.

"Yes," he said, "It will be nice if it's fine."

He told me that he had to walk the whole distance. He could not go by bicycle because he had to visit cottages and stock farms and small-holdings situated in places inaccessible to anyone but a pedestrian. His outward journey was twelve miles.

I joined him next morning. The country was at its best. The sun shone from a clear sky.

"The delivery is heavier than usual," he said, "It always is on a Saturday morning — especially at the beginning of a month."

On his round the postman was more off than on the narrow lanes that wind through the countryside. Through hunting gates, over stiles, through meadows haunted by Clun forest and Kerry Hill ewes and their lambs, and brown and white Hereford cattle, along the banks of the cool river, over foot bridges and stone bridges, jumping tributaries — that was the way we went. Everywhere we had a right of way, through cottage gardens flaming with bush and rambler roses, wallflowers, tulips, pansies, festoons of lilac, laburnum and chestnut trees, through stock yards strewn with fleeces recently shorn from sheep which bleated in pens waiting to be tar-marked with the farmer's brand, through springy meadows full of buttercups, clover, speedwell, cowslips and campion, beside woods carpeted with bluebells and haunted by rabbits and birds.

As we approached a lonely cottage a child would run out to greet the postman, and then, seeing me, retreat. These people, after long centuries, instinctively remember the Welsh marauders who came over the marches of Wales. That is why they are shy of strangers.

"Hallo, Nellie," he would say to the girl. "One for your mother."

The girl would reply shyly.

As we were about to pass on a disembodied voice would come from the interior of the cottage.

"Morning, Mr. Burns. Any news?"

"Nothing much. Bit of a fire up at James's farm."

A red faced woman of ample proportions, hot from the process of cleaning the hearth, would then appear at the door and demand details.

"Hope there inna bin much damage . . ."

The same happens at farms.

Sometimes the postman would tell a farm worker he met far out in the fields that he had left a letter for him at his home and from whom it had come! He prides himself on knowing the handwriting on every letter. He told me about a milkmaid who regularly had letters from her lover in a market town. She used in the beginning to send a reply by return, but as she knew the postman was aware of it, she became shy and sent her letters by hand to a distant post box.

Sometimes the postman has had to write replies to letters for illiterate people. In the Clee Hills three tribes of gipsies camp — the Smiths, Locks and Boswells. One of their number was in Shrewsbury Gaol. A warder wrote letters for him to his wife. The postman replied.

Everyone the postman meets asks for news from town. Most of them only see a weekly newspaper, which arrives by post. Many have never been in a cinema, or theatre, or visited London. The postman is the connecting link between these agricultural exiles and town. They ask him to mention them to their old friends. They urge him to retail the gossip going the round of the many little inns in the market town.

Sometimes a piece of gossip would cause us to linger on the doorstep of a cottage, and we could see inside.

They often had crude utilitarian furniture. Victorian prints, white owls, large as hens, caught in the countryside and stuffed. The living rooms had huge oak beams, faultily carved, and hung with hams and sides of bacon, white with flour and salt. On the sideboard were the inevitable hurricane lamps, and on rough cratches, made with hedge sticks, two or three old-fashioned fowling-pieces. In nearly every case, cottages and farms had cider cellars, the doors visible from outside, in which were hogshead casks and flagons of the beverage.

The delivery of letters finished at eleven o'clock, the postman was free until three, when he had to return by a specified route, selling stamps, collecting letters and parcels, and receiving orders for licences. The Post Office had provided him with a little hut in a field, apparently miles from anywhere. In this he could sleep during the interim between the delivery of letters and his return. In the winter, after having ploughed his way through deep snowdrifts, waded through the river in spate, gone through muddy fields, got drenched with rain or snow, he could dry his clothes and get warm. This hut was fitted with a desk, books, a seat, an oil stove and a small window. In a rack was a churchwarden's pipe from Broseley. The postmen on the other long walks are similarly provided for, but some cannot afford to waste their spare time, for the wages of the country postman are poor.

Between the end of the deliveries and the beginning of the collections of letters, these Clee Hill postmen take off the blue jacket of H. M. Postmaster-General and become gardeners or domestic servants at country houses, cleaning windows and silver, pruning trees, or trimming hedgerows. One man fitted up his hut with last, hammer and knives and stocked it with nails and leather. He became for three busy hours the cobbler for the countryside, and repaired the boots and shoes which were brought to him from long distances. The he tidied himself and became a postman again.

After a short rest at the hut, the postman and I walked into the nearest hamlet. We visited an old-world inn and had cider, made from apples grown in the local orchards and sold at threepence a pint, and we ate cottage-baked bread and local cheese. At three o'clock the return journey began by a specified route and the postman blew his whistle at arranged places and at given times. Not many people brought him letters or parcels. Country folk do not write much. One man, because he had not experienced the emotions of receiving a letter — he lived in a very remote part — wrote himself one and posted it in Cleobury. The postman, who realised what he had done, had to walk a mile through fields to deliver it.

On occasions the postman is asked by farmers to report signs of illness noticed in cattle or pigs, and to ask the vet in the market town for instructions. The vet generally sends back with the postman next day medicine and instructions for treatment. People living many miles from a shop often ask the postman to bring them articles in from town. A pretty milkmaid in a hamlet, who wished to attend a barn dance and impress the farm hands, once asked a postman if he would mind bringing her a pair of silk stockings!

Strange things happen to these walking post offices of the Clee Hills, these postmen who whistle and wait . . .

SIMON EVANS, THE SHROPSHIRE POSTMAN
by the Rev. H.E.G. Rope
(from *The Post* 17 August 1935)

A tall straight man, with a quick steady stride, blue-eyed, and healthy of colour, Mr. Simon Evans is a living testimony to the boon of open-air life. No one, on meeting him, would suspect that he had been gassed during the war, or that his life had been prescribed for him by doctors as well as natural bent. A close observer would, however, even without the name, divine the Welsh origin of this quiet unassuming local man.

Born amid the Welsh mountains, speaking Welsh as his mother-tongue, he has imbibed from childhood the Cymric inheritance, and though he went to school at eight in grim, grimy Birkenhead, he was never of the city, but remained undazzled, unattracted. The hard and searing war years, in which he fought and suffered so bravely, only deepened his disbelief in the vaunts of "Progress" thus terribly refuted. "The silence that is in the starry sky," the mountains, streams and trees amid which he was cradled haunted him; and he loved and understood children. Indeed some of his most touching and thoughtful pictures portray the sunshine of childhood amid the gloom of war-time, reminding me of certain scenes in Fr. Owen Dudley's "The Shadow on the Earth."

The Celts and Poetry

I remember, as a stripling, travelling between Aberystwyth and Shrewsbury with a drover, who told me he was a Welsh bard. This made a great impression on me, since English farmers, with all their sterling qualities, are seldom poets. There is a vein of poetry in most Celtic country folk, surely, and Simon Evans is certainly a poet born. I think many of his readers will share my regret that his last book contains none of the lyrics so happily interspersed in "Round the Crooked Steeple." We hope he will give us more of this kind. The present eclipse of poetry will pass; it is passing already.

Like John Clare, William Barnes and many another, Simon Evans completed his own education, reading widely and variously, avoiding the danger of smothering his own gifts, while sound instinct and good judgement kept him away from the trivial and the worthless. A good craftsman quickly recognises good work from bad.

His keen observation and genial, yet detached, humour has made this son of Wales the Hardy of the Shropshire region, between the Clees and the Worcestershire border, where he settled some time after the War, a region untouched by Mary Webb and hardly known to A. E. Housman. He came just in the nick of time to preserve in record a local life and local character and colour that will very soon, I fear, have vanished. All-levelling mechanisation is gaining ground daily. The skilled cobbler and leather worker, with whom he lodged two or three years ago, died and left no one to carry on the craft. Elderly people as well as young are among those driven away by the economic stress. I can hardly take a walk to-day without coming upon gateposts, cartwheels, nay whole wagons, built to last for generations, calmly left to rot and make way for their hideous supplanters; forges closed down, or new blisters of corrugated iron broken out upon the landscape, or a new massacre of what trees and spinneys yet remain. Indeed I think my gifted neighbour is only half aware, if that, of the extent and speed of the destruction. Doubtless it is better so; else he could hardly write so cheerfully. He has been signally successful in tracing out those who still inherit the traditions of an English England, the local homely simplicities so blindly scorned by the bright young things. One of his Clee Hill characters died only the other day. The enemies of tradition are carrying all before them at present.

A Kindly Humour

Our author's rise to fame has been rapid and deserved. His gifts are undoubtedly great. To poetic imagination he adds rare powers of observation and portrayal of his fellow-men, enhanced by a kindly Dickensian humour.

And now I will permit myself a word of criticism. The chief defect of his work is the absence of a consistent philosophy of life. At the same time, it shows a growing consciousness of this lack, an attempt to make it good. One who has seen and been through so much suffering must needs touch upon life's deeper problems. Nature-worship, like patriotism, is not enough, and his last book half admits this; it even concedes that nature witnesses to Almighty Power, but does not follow up the admission. The proposed new religion of beauty is not religion; it is admiration, but not worship. Beauty is but one aspect of creation, reflecting the attribute of Almighty Power. Created beauty is no more self-explaining or self-existent than nature itself. What is the ultimate meaning of the universe, of man and his part in it? The question is evaded, an evasion great and enduring work cannot afford. Another question, "What think ye of Christ?" is put aside altogether as if it were of no importance.

If human life has no ultimate meaning, then "what is it all but the trouble of ants in the gleam of a million million suns?" Now, Simon Evans is not a fatalist, like Hardy; he is free from the morbid obsession that blemishes the work of Mary Webb (notably in "Gone to Earth"). To put by momentous questions which demand an answer is no part of wisdom. I think the Shropshire postman is approaching the same conclusion, and that his future work will go deeper into life's greatest issues, all the more so since the local vein he has worked so ably nears exhaustion.

Among his greatest gifts is that of sympathy. Although in some ways mentally aloof (inevitably) from the young generation whose illusions he never shared or could share, Simon Evans is the most companionable of men, easily adapting himself to the company he is with, altogether a kind neighbourly man gifted with "the excellence of sincerity and strength," local without narrowness, unspoiled by success, unchanged by celebrity, a modest, courteous, and most friendly fellow pilgrim on life's journey.

13: Simon, 9 March 1940. (Mr F. Morrison)

Mr. Simon Evans, the postman-author, of Cleobury Mortimer, died early yesterday in the Queen Elizabeth Hospital, Birmingham, from an illness arising out of his service in the Great War. He was in his fortyfifth year.

Simon Evans, whose writings on country life won him a reputation among lovers of nature far beyond Shropshire, where he had spent the last twenty years, had an unusual career. He was born on a lonely farm in Montgomeryshire. When he was six years old and unable to speak or understand a word of English, his family migrated to Birkenhead. He served in the Army in the Great War, and was wounded and badly gassed. When discharged, he was told his only hope of recovery lay in an open-air occupation. Thus it was he chose to enter the service of the Post Office as a rural letter-carrier at Cleobury Mortimer. His round was in the sparsely populated Rea Valley, where he lived close to nature with his books in the kindly fellowship of the country folk he loved.

It was here that he first began to write, with no thought of publishing his work until the suggestion was made to him by a tutor of Ruskin College. Then followed several volumes of essays, character sketches, pictures of the Clee Hill country, and tales of Border folk — "Round About the Crooked Steeple" (1931), "At Abda [sic] Burf" (1932) and "More Tales from Round About the Crooked Steeple" (1935), "Applegarth" (1936) and "Shropshire Days and Shropshire Ways" (1938). He was also an occasional contributor to "The Birmingham Post" and "Mail". While it has been said of him that his literary reputation was due less to the merit of what he wrote than to the fact that he was inspired to write, it has also been said that few writers have ever come near enough to the authentic countryman to reproduce his idiom and psychology with the same easy fidelity.

A correspondent writes:-

Some few years ago I rented a summer bungalow in Cleobury Mortimer. I became interested in the postman who delivered the letters there. I used to see him at four o'clock in the afternoon returning from an eighteen miles walk — nine miles out and nine miles return, with two hours rest. This postman was Simon Evans. Something should be said of his appearance, because he was an unusual type. He was 6ft. 2in. or 3in. in height, magnificently built, with blue eyes and reddish curly hair; altogether he was a man whose carriage and appearance would attract attention. He was one of a family the members of which for generations were known as the Red Giants. His was a vigorous and rugged personality, and he had a simplicity of character which endeared him to all. Perhaps he can better be described as having the heart of a child. Moreover, he had the poetic temperament of a true Welshman.

His marriage was a romance. He frequently broadcast, and met at the B.B.C.

the lady he married. He was a Clee county enthusiast and she a Cotswold enthusiast (she is a native of Burford). The acquaintance ripened and they were married two years ago. When he proposed she would not believe he was a rural postman, pointing out, among other things, that he was wearing most expensive brogues. He had some difficulty in persuading her of the truth of his statement. They were an ideal couple, she vivacious and accomplished and he the most companionable and sympathetic of men.

OBITUARY
from *The Countryman* Jan/Mar 1941

. . . I am really sorry to hear of the death of Simon Evans, the postman author and broadcaster. You will perhaps recall his autobiographical article which appeared a little more than two years ago. He came to the office several times. He had character and a single heart, intelligence and a manly bearing, and was, as he said to me, 'a true countryman'. The good notices his half-dozen books received did not spoil him. He remained an honest postman and a plucky one, for he always felt the results of that gassing he had in the last War which finally carried him off. Here is a good man as the public saw him on his rounds. 'I feel that there are so many people who do not know how much pleasure can be theirs by simply looking at the hills, walking in the wind and listening to the music of a little river', is a remark he makes in one of his letters. In the autumn of 1939 his gas trouble compelled him to give up his work as a postman. 'I must earn, somehow, about £2 a week', he wrote to me. 'It sounds very little. But a sure £100 a year is not easy to find.'